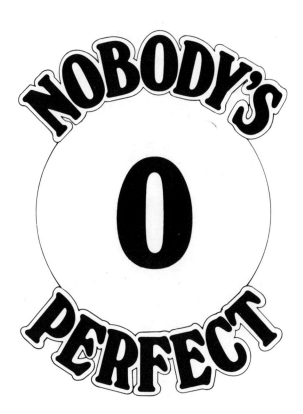

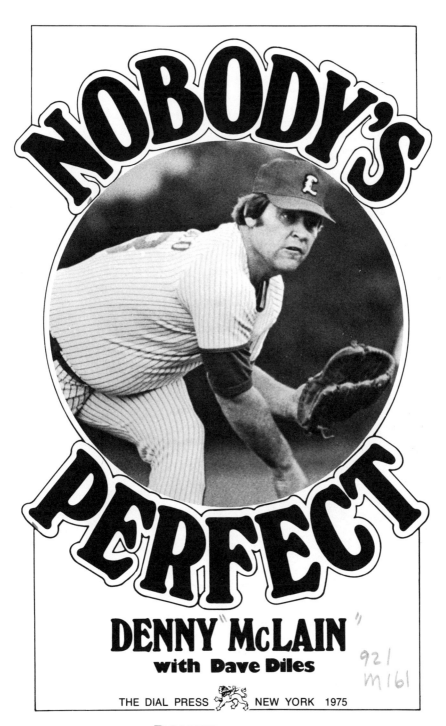

NOBODY'S PERFECT

DENNY "McLAIN"
with Dave Diles

THE DIAL PRESS NEW YORK 1975

Manufactured in the United States of America
First printing, 1975

Photo facing title page used by permission of Wide World Photos.
Photo on title page by Sam McLeod, The London Free Press.

Library of Congress Catalog Card Number: 75–7541
ISBN: 0-8037-5758-1

For my part, I dedicate this book to my wife Sharyn, who has endured more than any human being should have to and given me far more than I have deserved.

Denny McLain

. . . my part, I dedicate to Lois, Phyllis, Marge, and Bill, who understand 'most everything about me, and love me even when they don't understand.

Dave Diles

We gratefully acknowledge the assistance of the Detroit Tiger Baseball Club, and in particular General Manager Jim Campbell and Director of Public Relations Hal Middlesworth. A special word of thanks also is due Marge Mitchell, Carolyn Francis, and Valerie Tangert, who labored many hours over the tape recordings. Most especially, our thanks go to four McLain children and two Diles children, who gave up time.

—The Authors

To those who do not understand,
no explanation is sufficient;
to those who do understand,
no explanation is necessary.

—Author unknown

INTRODUCTION

A book by, or about, Dennis Dale McLain had been kicked around before, by a lot of different people for a lot of different reasons.

We had not seen each other for nearly a year when he called and suggested we get together. When we did, he had that crooked grin on his face. He looked older, especially around the eyes. Little wonder. For the past few years, Denny McLain had done everything but sleep. He was fat—not just a little overweight, but downright fat. His belly hung down over his belt and he looked for all the world like one of those afternoon beer drinkers who wears his pants just above the crotch.

It was early in February 1974 that we met. We had arranged by phone to meet at Denny's office to discuss the possibility of a book. "It'll be dynamite," he promised. "I want to spill my guts out and tell the truth about everything."

It was a raw day, typically Michigan, for February. As I sat there waiting for him to come out of his private office, I thought of the sick line that it'd be a cold day when Denny and I got together on time for anything.

The office was in Southfield, just a few blocks from where he once had lived, and another few blocks from another office he had occupied when he was throwing hard, living fast, and rolling high. These days, Denny was throwing nothing but bull, rolling with the punches, and merely trying to figure out ways to live high again.

But some things never change.

In the outer office, the desk was littered with seven empty Pepsi bottles. Notes cluttered the receptionist's desk. A note pad bore the lettering, "From the desk of Denny McLain, vice president."

The door to his office was slightly ajar when I arrived and he yelled out to wait, that he'd be only a minute. It turned into forty-five, but with Denny a minute can be an eternity. On the other hand, he can turn a whole night into a fleeting thing. Even a career.

Finally the meeting broke up and Denny McLain, vice president of whatever, summoned me into his office. I had known him since the day he came to the Detroit Tigers in 1963. He was a kid of nineteen.

With that crooked grin, he somehow looked the same

eleven years later. What an ornery kid! In a way, he looked nineteen. In another, he looked nineteen multiplied by plenty. The fast balls he dared them to hit, the broads and the late hours, the plane rides and the joy rides, the days on end with no sleep, the crap tables in Las Vegas and the hot nights in Shreveport, the fast-buck deals and the promises unfulfilled—all of these helped make Dennis Dale McLain an old man before his time, a baseball has-been on a day when he should have had the whole world in the palm of his hand.

Denny asked me to wait a minute or two longer. He had an urgent telephone call to make. Every phone call was forever urgent. And why not wait for him? Didn't everybody? Always? Why should February 9, 1974, be different from all other days?

As he turned away, I noticed his shirttail was hanging out. Funny, here's a guy who could manage to look rumpled in a $500 suit.

That's where it all started. We went from there to everywhere, meeting in all sorts of places at all sorts of hours. Three nights after that first meeting, I sat in a lounge and watched Denny and his group perform. Even counting fat folks twice, there were no more than 120 people in the joint.

Denny started out by singing "I Gotta Be Me." His was a nervous voice and there were some high notes he didn't quite reach. Right in the middle of the song some loudmouth yelled for him to sing "When the Saints Go Marchin' In," but Denny pretended he didn't hear him.

A drunk broad at ringside asked Denny if he could sing "Filipino Baby." Denny never heard of the song, nor of Cowboy Copas. He sang lines like, "I took the blows, and did it my way," and ". . . regrets, I've had a few," but there were only two, maybe three, people in the audience who knew how painful those lines must have been for him.

It was an agonizing evening and there was no end to the humiliation. Here was a man who had played the organ since he was six years old—and he plays it pretty well—but that night he could have had Lanza's voice, Lenny Dee's fingers, and Burt Reynolds's body, and it wouldn't have mattered. What crowd there was paid little attention. Denny got scorn and disdain and precious little else. Later in the engagement, the crowds, the act, and the response got better, but he no longer was hot off a thirty-one-victory season; he had not won a World Series game since 1968; most of the publicity since those days had been bad. He commanded neither the price nor the attention of the good old days. Here he was, not quite thirty years old and he was through. And they let him know it.

There was a lady at the next table and she had too much makeup, a bad bleach job, and a dress—well, all she needed to make the getup complete was a calliope. Her drinking had put her in that terrible in-between stage: She had consumed too much to be quiet and too little to pass out.

I was applauding as Denny finished a number and she turned on me and wanted to know, "Why in the hell are you clapping? He's terrible!"

My explanation to her—and to this day I don't know why I ever bother to try and reason with a drunk—was that I was his friend, and that I wanted to encourage him. My ear isn't made out of tin and it had occurred to me Denny's group was no immediate threat to The Beatles.

I could have explained to her that in eleven years I had seen every side of this fellow. I have seen him unbeatable on the mound and unbearable in the clubhouse; I have seen him drive all night to visit a dying kid, and then be unkind to his best friends; I have seen him try to make a fast buck, and give his last one to a bum on the street.

He is a man (and sometimes I am still tempted to call him a boy) who can make you love him to pieces and hate him to death—often in the same day, sometimes in the same sentence. As long as I have known him, the only thing predictable about Dennis Dale McLain has been his unpredictability, the only thing consistent, his inconsistency.

Denny has never been dull.

Maybe in another quarter century folks will make up their minds whether they love him or hate him. Chances are, people still will be talking about him then, because there will never be another like him.

This is his story, as best he remembers it and the way he sees it, as best I can write it.

Dave Diles

CONTENTS

ON TOP OF

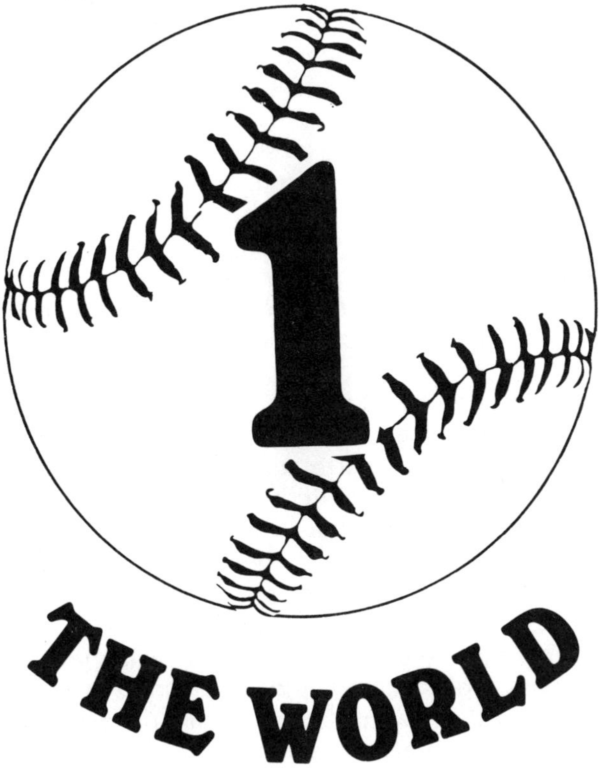

THE WORLD

I never asked to be a hero. When you think about it, maybe I never was. In many respects, I was more antihero than anything else. Even when I was winning more baseball games than anyone in thirty years, I heard as many boos as cheers.

When I look back—and I do that quite a bit—I try to reconcile myself to all that jeering by recalling that I pitched most of my baseball games in a town loaded with rowdies. In any town, the great majority of the fans, of any sport, are good people. It's just that in Detroit, the few bad ones are so rotten they sometimes make it difficult to remember the good.

Detroit is a town that threw snowballs and iceballs at a pro football coach. It's a town whose fans kayoed an umpire with an empty booze bottle. It's a town whose ruffians tore out seats and threw them at opposing outfielders.

Some of the idiots threw so many nuts and bolts and nails and firecrackers and smoke bombs and pieces of pipe at the players that the rights to salvage the junk in Tiger Stadium would have made a man a millionaire.

I always get my best ideas too late. I should have quit when I was hot back in 1968 and 1969 and gotten into the junk business. Come to think of it, that's pretty much what I did when the zip went out of my fast ball.

It's been said plenty of times that the baseball fans of Detroit carried on a love-hate relationship with me. I'll buy that. I feel the same way about them. If they couldn't understand me, it's little wonder. At the time, I hardly understood me either. Things were happening so fast I had neither the time nor the inclination to figure out why—for me it was how much and how soon.

I never set out to be "great." All I did was throw as hard as I could for as long as I could, and try to win as many games as I could. The fact that I won fifty-five of them in two seasons was my achievement and at the same time my undoing.

Funny thing, I don't really remember very many of them. I've been accused of putting pitching last on my list of priorities. That's a bunch of crap and anybody idiotic enough even to think that ought to be put away somewhere, for keeps. How could anyone win fifty-five games in two seasons, even three, and not have a great degree of concentration on baseball? I know I was involved in a ton of outside activities. Too many, for sure. But I was shrewd enough to figure out that without baseball, most of these other things would never have happened.

0

The opportunities, the resultant temptations—and my being overcome by them—were a direct by-product of my pitching skills.

And for a time, I was damned skillful.

As I look back—and don't kid yourself, everyone does that—I still am amazed that I could do all the things I did and avoid a total physical and emotional collapse. What was it Satchel Paige once said about never looking back because something might be gaining on you?

Thank God I never looked back in the glory years. For one thing, it would have broken my concentration, and on most things my concentration span is about eight seconds. For another, if I had been able to see exactly what was happening, I surely could have avoided some of the pitfalls. But what the hell, it wouldn't have been nearly so exciting.

Now, if by chance you are a psychiatrist or a psychologist or one of those other people who try to peer into people's minds, you'd better put this book down right now. Read any more and I'll have *you* on the couch. First off, most of you guys are a little bit out of touch with reality, say by about three million light years. But let's come back to this stuff later.

The seasons of 1968 and 1969 were so good as to be almost unreal (in some ways I wish they had been) and even though these years made everything else possible, I am staggered when I recount them. It's even more staggering when I hear and read the accounts of some of my critics—and I could count them on the fingers of the Mormon Tabernacle Choir.

But critics are critics, in the main, out of necessity. Most of the writers who chronicle the activities of athletes can't walk and chew gum at the same time. A couple I've encountered must get their only thrill in life by looking at naked athletes in showers and locker rooms.

A fellow named John Gordy used to play some mighty good football for the Detroit Lions, and a newspaperman once reminded John that "the pen is mightier than the sword." And John said, "That's true, unless you happen to be in a sword fight."

Most of my battles with writers, broadcasters, and fans have been the nonsword variety, although there are a few I'd like to duel.

Even when I was pitching better than anyone else in baseball, I couldn't silence my critics. They surely will be out in full

0

force and voice once they read this and that's fine because now it's my turn to tell my story like it really happened.

Let's start at spring training 1968. I had no reason to suspect that I was going to win thirty-one baseball games, nor that the Detroit Tigers would win the pennant. If I were a betting man (and I am, you know) I would have bet cash money that the Tigers couldn't win the pennant. Frankly, looking back on it, I think we must have done it with mirrors. There were several teams with better talent.

I'll go into great detail about the 1967 season in another chapter—but the Tigers should have won the American League pennant that year. Had I not been pissed off at the manager, Mayo Smith (and he was mildly perturbed at me), we would have won the damned thing. We had it right in the palms of our hands and we blew it.

When I say we, I mean myself and Mayo Smith. Of course, we had a lot of help from Hank Aguirre, who was the greatest reverse triple-threat I've ever seen in baseball. Whether Hank was more pitiful as a pitcher, fielder, or hitter is a question that will baffle baseball experts for generations to come. All he had to do was think, one time, in one baseball game in his life, then the Tigers would have won the American League pennant in 1967. Thinking is another thing Hank didn't do well.

We were playing the California Angels in consecutive doubleheaders on Saturday and Sunday, the final two days of the season. All we had to do was win three of the four games. We won the opener on Saturday, then lost the second game because when the Angels had the bases loaded and no one out, Aguirre fielded a grounder hit back to the mound, and for reasons that only he could understand, threw the ball to first base!

We split again on Sunday, Joe Sparma winning the first game. I started the second one and got kayoed in the third inning after giving up three runs and four hits. It was no consolation then, or now, that I was not charged with the defeat. We lost. That's all that counts.

The main point is, I should have been pitching earlier, and could have won at least a game or two. Then we wouldn't have faced such a critical situation on the last weekend of the season.

This is another of those things that I will detail later, but I had missed six or seven pitching turns because of an ankle injury. There have been all sorts of wild stories told about how it

0

happened, but the truth is that it was a common, household accident. I was sleeping on the couch when suddenly I was awakened by a noise in our garage. The garbage cans were being turned over and our dog Pepsi was barking his fool head off. I jumped up and ran toward the door leading into the garage.

What I didn't know was that my foot was asleep. I turned my ankle, sprained my foot, and tore some ligaments in it. It's as simple as that. Some of the better stories circulated were that I kicked a stool in the locker room and that a Mafia don stomped on me. They make great stories, except they're simply not true.

There was no way I could pitch for two or three weeks. But I had been good about getting my treatments regularly, since I was hurt in late August. The team was in Washington and I went to Manager Mayo Smith and told him I thought maybe I could pitch. I had been throwing the ball and knew I could land on my feet after throwing it, and I thought I could pitch over the pain and get some people out and help the Tigers win the thing. I told Mayo I thought I could pitch in the weekend series against the Senators. Hell, I could beat them pitching from a wheelchair!

Mayo dismissed me quickly. "Fuck it," he said. "I already have my pitching rotation set for the Washington series."

I didn't care for his sarcasm, so I didn't say another word to him. He put me in the bullpen during that Saturday doubleheader against the Angels and I was up and down throwing in four different innings.

After we split on Saturday, he came up to me after the game and said, "You'll start the second game tomorrow."

"Jesus, Mayo," I said, "I pitched thirty or thirty-five minutes in the bullpen today. I'm whipped. I don't think I could get my old maid aunt out with the stuff I have left."

Mayo just turned and walked away. As it turned out he was right and so was I. I started, like he said, and I couldn't have gotten my old maid aunt out, like I said.

Even though we had come so close in 1967, there was no legitimate reason to suspect that we could win it in 1968. We couldn't run and we couldn't throw anybody out. I mean, we were slower than the fog off manure. If you put our players in a race against a tree, you'd naturally have to bet on the tree.

Our pitching was iffy, and as far as we knew our hitting was no more than adequate. I'll say this for Mayo Smith: He knew that club's strong and weak points and he managed it ex-

5

0

tremely well. He knew the only way to win was to sit there and wait for those guys to hit. I doubt that Mayo ever kidded himself about that team, and if you ask him today, he'll tell you it was just one of those things with a team simply putting it all together for one big splash, a splash never to happen again.

In a way, I'm glad it happened just once. I'm sure I couldn't have taken it a second time.

In 1967 we had won twenty more games than we lost, and had to settle for a tie for second place. Maybe most of our players felt that season proved we could do it, and perhaps some of them felt that all we needed was a little extra push to go all the way in 1968.

Not me. I think I always have been able to look at my teams objectively—even dating back to high school—and as I looked at the 1968 edition of the Detroit Tigers I saw a team that would win a few more than it would lose. But the pennant? We'd need a ton of breaks. After all, Willie Horton had been hobbling around with an assortment of injuries in 1967 (and, in truth, it didn't take a whole lot to make Willie hobble); Al Kaline had batted .308, but he was getting up in years; Norm Cash was almost as old as Al (even by Norm's own count) and he was slipping at the plate and had batted just .242 in 1967; Mickey Stanley was coming off a .210 season at bat; Don Wert was struggling to bat .260; and neither Mickey Lolich nor myself had proved we could win twenty.

Hell, I was just the fourth starter when we went to camp that spring. I was behind Mickey Lolich, Earl Wilson, and Joe Sparma, and I had more confidence in me than anyone else. I came out of spring training throwing the ball well, that's all I remember. I thought I'd have a good year, but no one ever thinks he can win thirty-one unless he's a babbling idiot.

At the start of the season I won five in a row, and, truthfully, I don't remember much of anything about those games. I doubt that anyone took much notice of it, even though our team was off to a good start and in first place. That sometimes happened with the Tigers, but they generally did a complete fold so no one was too excited about the good start we had. But in 1968 we didn't fold. We got into first place, to stay, on May 10 when I won a game at Washington 12–1—it was my fifth straight—and we never left that spot.

My wife Sharyn saved all the clippings over the years—the good and the bad—but even we didn't start to fret over having every single blurb until I had won ten or twelve.

0

I remember when I won my sixth game I beat Jim Merritt of the Minnesota Twins for the second time in that young season. In fact, all season I never did lose a game to the Twins.

The secret to beating them, I found, was to pitch around Tony Oliva. I'd sooner walk him than give him a good pitch to hit. And I didn't lose a single game on the West Coast. Of course, everything out there is conducive to good pitching— the cool nights and in general a happy environment.

One incident sticks out in my mind on our first trip to California that season. I was in my hotel room and there was a knock on my door in the middle of the afternoon. I was lying around in my shorts so I didn't bother to put my pants on when I answered the door. There, in front of me, stood a young goddess of about twenty-three and she was carrying a package.

"This is for you," she said. "Wear it in good health."

And as quickly as she said it, she was gone.

I figured no good-looking thing like that is going to drop a bomb off in my room, so I opened the package and in it was a beautiful lounging robe. And damned if I didn't wear it in good health, and good luck, and in lots of other situations.

Several weeks later the club was in Boston, and after a night game several of us got into a card game. Myself, Gates Brown, Pat Dobson, Willie Horton, Dick McAuliffe, Jim Northrup, John Hiller, and maybe a couple more players were having a pretty good go at it. Naturally, I was lounging in my new robe.

I had beaten Northrup five or six straight hands of seven-card high-low and Jim had consumed a couple of drinks and was a little bent out of shape. Northrup could never handle his booze anyway. He's the kind of drinker who'd get high just thinking about going to a bar.

Anyway, I was rubbing it into him about beating him, and he reached across the table and ripped my new robe. I lit on him like the green on grass and gave him a quick punch in the face. It was all over, just like that; Gates jumped in and stopped the fight.

Jim won lots of games for me with long balls, but I couldn't stand him then and can't stand him now.

I remember I won my thirteenth game in Cleveland on June 24. Alvin Dark was managing the Indians and they were a pretty hot club about that time and the fans were rattling on about winning the pennant. We stopped that ridiculous talk, but not

0

until the Indians had beaten us three straight in a long five-game weekend series. Eddie Fisher, Steve Hargan, and Luis Tiant had quickly reduced our lead from eight and one-half games to five and one-half, coming into the last two games of the series.

But my old buddy Joe Sparma beat the Indians 4–1, even with Sudden Sam McDowell pitching for them. Then I won the finale 14–3. If I remember correctly, Northrup hit a couple of grand slams that day, and our lead was back up to seven and one-half games. Not bad for a mediocre team late in June.

By the All-Star Game break, my record was 16–2.

I had been selected for the game, and so had my catcher, Bill Freehan. I pitched the first game of a doubleheader in Oakland on July 7 and won the game 5–4. I had made arrangements for a jet plane to take me to the All-Star Game, and Freehan had indicated he'd like to go along.

So I waited around until he finished catching the second game.

The deal was this, plain and simple: I had the use of the jet, but I had to pay the expenses. So I took Sharyn and some friends of ours, Don and Alice Matthews, and Freehan decided to take his wife. We had planned to stop off in Las Vegas—after all, how much out of the way can Vegas be from anywhere?

Freehan asked me in front what it would cost him, and I explained I thought the fair thing would be for him to give me what his airline fare would be. And I said, "If you want to chip in with anything else, I wouldn't turn it down."

We not only stopped in Las Vegas *before* the game, but afterward as well. One of the things I recall about that trip was that we were flying at 41,000 feet and we could see Vegas when we were 175 miles away. It was just that clear and beautiful, and it was one of the most peaceful times of my entire life.

I never hit the bed the whole time there—either time there, for that matter. I gambled all night, all day, then all night again, then took off for Houston. One of our pilots was a twenty-two-year-old kid named Dennis Lewis and we had a strange envy of each other: He envied me because I was a big winner and a high roller, and I envied him because he could fly the hell out of that jet.

We got to Houston at about two in the afternoon (after all, it was a night game) and checked in. I threw down a Pepsi and some deviled eggs, and went to the ball park where I stumbled through two innings and gave up just one hit and no runs.

0

We asked Freehan if he wanted to make the trip back with us—stopping in Vegas, of course, then flying the other people to Detroit before rejoining the Tigers in Minnesota. Bill declined. I guess that's what a college education does for you.

The upshot of the whole trip was that I won about $4,000 at the tables, the jet cost me $9,000 and Freehan never came up with a penny. Bill's educated, but cheap.

I hadn't slept in days and was living on "greenies" and even popped a couple before I pitched two nights later in Minnesota (I won, incidentally, 5–1, beating my old friend Jim Kaat).

The Tigers still were in front by six and seven games and I still couldn't believe it. We just had no business being in first place, but damned if we weren't right there. Every time I checked the standings in the newspaper, there we were. And Lolich wasn't winning all that much—he wound up winning seventeen, but he didn't get rolling until mid-August and wound up winning ten of his last twelve decisions.

But the other teams were eliminating themselves. Baltimore was hurting and no one else could get a streak going.

It's difficult to believe, but I don't remember much at all about those games I was winning. I had lost only three games the night I went for my nineteenth, and I do remember that. It was July 23 in Washington and the losing pitcher was Phil Ortega, who had broken in with the Dodgers.

Four days later at Baltimore I absolutely knew for sure I would win number twenty. I knew it warming up, and I told Freehan there was no way anyone would beat me that night. I had superstuff, struck out seven, and threw nothing but fast balls the last three or four innings.

My twenty-fifth victory I remember, too. It was at Boston against Jim Lonborg and I had to struggle through the early innings. I've often said that in this game, I pitched the best single inning of baseball I ever pitched in my life. Somewhere in the middle of the game, Lonborg led off with a chopper down the left field line for a double. Someone else got an infield hit and stole second. There I was, in a tight game, with runners at second and third and no one out. Staring me in the face were Dalton Jones, who's always been tough for me to get out, and Carl Yastrzemski, and Kenny Harrelson, who were tough for everybody.

I just figured, "Fuck it, if they're gonna beat me, they're gonna have to hit my fast ball."

0

I whipped three straight past Jones, got two strikes on Yastrzemski right away before he fouled a couple off, then I fanned him. Now, Harrelson always was a good hitter, but somehow I had uncommon success with him. If Kenny had six hits off me in his life, then that's twice as many as I think he got.

Now I've worked my way two-thirds of the way out of trouble, and out comes the manager, Mayo Smith. I needed him out there like a sore arm, and I already had one of those.

"Walk him."

Those were Mayo's orders.

"Fuck him."

That was my reply to Mayo.

Hell, I had made some tremendous pitches to Jones and Yastrzemski, both left-handed hitters, throwing everything into what I've always called "the black," that part of the strike zone that pitchers love and batters hate.

All in all, Mayo and I had a pretty good relationship and I could always talk to him, and man, did I talk to him that night.

"You've listened to me and let me pitch my way for twenty-four god-damned victories, and I'm gonna pitch to this guy. Hell, Mayo, Harrelson couldn't hit me if he knew in advance what I was gonna throw."

And I explained that Rico Petrocelli was on deck and he hit me like he owned me. Mayo just turned and walked away. He didn't say anything else, but he could have been arrested for what he was thinking.

Freehan went behind the plate and Harrelson stepped in. Now, remember I hadn't thrown a thing except a fast ball to the two previous batters. Harrelson never saw a fast ball. I fed him three straight sliders, all of them in the black, down and away, and he never moved a muscle. Just stood there.

I was so thrilled I wanted to jump up and down on the mound. Folks were talking about my winning thirty and it was one of the great feelings of all time.

Right then and there I knew I would win thirty. Hell, it was only August 16.

Damned if I didn't lose two in a row, 10–2 to the White Sox and 2–1 to the Yankees. I gave up nine of the runs to the White Sox and it didn't console me that, because of a lot of errors, only two of the runs were earned. We lost, and I lost, and those were the things that counted. By then the pennant was within

0

our grasp and winning thirty meant lots of dollar bills in Denny's pockets.

The loss to the Yankees came in the first inning when Roy White hit a two-run home run off me. I was pretty good at giving up home runs. Willie Horton hit one for us in the seventh inning, but we couldn't get anything else off Mel Stottlemyre.

Next time out I managed to beat California (which I did five times that year) then went against Baltimore trying for my twenty-seventh. We were at home and had more than forty thousand out for a Sunday afternoon game.

I didn't have a nickel's worth of stuff for the first four innings, but an amazingly lucky play in the early going turned the ball game around for me. The Orioles had the bases loaded, no one out, and Boog Powell the hitter. Now, I used to sit up at night trying to figure out ways to retire Boog Powell, and nothing ever worked. He could hit me if I shot the ball through a cannon and he had a toothpick for a bat.

He creamed one back at me and I thought I was dead. Somehow I got my glove up in time and caught the ball, threw it to Ray Oyler at third, and he threw it to Norm Cash at first for a triple play. It happened so fast we could have gotten four outs before Boog got out of the box. I got better after that, and we won the game 7–3.

We were in California when I won my twenty-ninth and an eerie thing happened. I had a 7–2 lead when I went out to pitch the bottom of the ninth and all of a sudden people in the stands stood up and started cheering. First thought in my mind was that the President had walked in, so I called Cash over from first base and asked him what the commotion was all about.

"That's for you, big fellow, all for you."

I had goose bumps all over my body. I think I struck out two batters in that inning. The juices were flowing so hard through me after all that applause I could have thrown the baseball through concrete.

I won my thirtieth on September 14 and strangely enough I can't remember much about the game. There was so much bullshit going on before the game that the contest was almost secondary. I drove to the park myself because Sharyn was coming down later. We had a ton of people at our house.

The hassle started as soon as I hit the parking lot in Tiger Stadium. First off, the game was on national television, and

0

despite that we had more than forty thousand fans in the stands.

I knew there was no way to get any time to myself, so I figured, "Screw it, I'll talk to everybody." And everybody wanted to talk.

"What did you have for breakfast?"

I've had the same breakfast for thirty years—eggs up, bacon or sausage, toast, orange juice, and milk. And wash it all down with a Pepsi.

"Did you sleep well last night?"

Certainly. All I have to do to sleep is go to bed. Problem is, most nights I wasn't bothering to go to bed. But I had gone home the night before, played the organ for a while, watched a little television, and hit the sack. Slept like a baby.

They asked me everything except what kind of toilet paper I used.

Dizzy Dean, the last pitcher to win thirty, was there. He came over and wished me luck and we posed for pictures.

When it came time for me to go out and warm up, I felt like someone lifted an organ off my shoulders. Hell, that was the only peace and quiet I had had all day long. I wanted to warm up at noon just to get away from people.

Chuck Dobson was the Oakland starter, but Diego Segui wound up the loser. I was plenty pissed off at Mayo for not starting Al Kaline. How in the name of sense could you leave Kaline out of the starting lineup?

As for the game itself, I remember hanging a couple of curve balls to Reggie Jackson and we trailed 4–3 going into the bottom of the ninth. Kaline finally got up as a pinch hitter and walked, and I knew then we would win the game. We got two runs and won it 5–4, and all I remember then was leaping out of the dugout with Kaline on my shoulder when Horton got the game-winning hit.

The pennant had been won, but this was the frosting on the cake.

The easiest part of 1968 was the pitching. That was pretty simple most of the time, but the rest of it was hell. Having to cater to everybody. Everybody wanting something. Don't get me wrong, I'd do it again because it was a once-in-a-lifetime experience and I enjoyed it. But it was a tedious and trying time in a lot of ways.

Wouldn't you know, I even screwed up the postgame celebration?

0

Sharyn had invited lots of people to a big party at the house, and the hero shows up at 9:30 P.M. The party had been in progress for three and one-half hours!

Some folks from California had flown in to meet with me about a possible television movie, and I decided that being with them to talk business and bullshit after my thirtieth victory was more important than being with family and friends. Somehow I've managed always to foul up my priorities.

Decisions, decisions, I had tons of them. I couldn't avoid them even on the ball field. I started forty-one games that year, and only four times was there a no-decision.

We still had thirteen games to go after my thirtieth, but I didn't pitch all that much. I got number thirty-one on the nineteenth against the Yankees (that's when I deliberately served up a gopher ball to Mickey Mantle; I'll tell all about that in another chapter), and we laughed all the way to the World Series.

Mayo asked me if I wanted to pitch on a Wednesday and I told him no. I had a terrible cold.

"I ain't gonna pitch tomorrow, Mayo, and if I don't feel like it I won't pitch the next day. From now on, I'm running this club."

And I propped my feet up on his desk and sat in his chair. We all laughed about it then.

The night we clinched the pennant there were parties everywhere, but I wound up with a small group of friends at a bar in Dearborn in the western suburbs. When I got home about one thirty in the morning my yard was a mess, toilet paper all over the place. The players had sort of partied by themselves, and General Manager Jim Campbell had been nice enough to entertain the wives. Sharyn wasn't at all mad when I got home. After all, how many times does a guy win thirty-one and help win a pennant?

I should have won thirty-two.

The next-to-last day of the season I pitched against Washington. I went seven innings and shut the Senators out with just two hits when Mayo told me I'd had enough.

"You've pitched enough for one season. Just take it easy."

Jesus, but I was mad. What's two more lousy innings? Besides, I could win another game and what's so wrong about that?

But Mayo had his way this time and brought in the old cross-seamer, Don McMahon, and he proceeded to give up two runs and we lost the frigging game 2–1. It wasn't so much the number of victories I had, but the mere fact that I loved to win. Mayo and I had a pretty good go-round about it in the dugout, and his argument was that he just wanted to give some of the other pitchers some work.

"Why?" I bellowed. "They haven't worked all season. Why work 'em now?"

The World Series that followed was anticlimactic.

We had won the American League pennant by a dozen games—first time the Tigers had won the thing in twenty-three years. The town went crazy. We didn't hit the last week of the season, scoring only fourteen runs in our last seven games. I think most of us were dragged out when the so-called autumn classic opened in St. Louis on October 2. I know I was, and I showed it.

I didn't have much in the opening game but it wouldn't have mattered, anyway. Bob Gibson stuck our bats in our behinds, striking out seventeen—and Gibby said afterward his arm hurt all the time in three places and the pain never goes away. Hell, I knew exactly how he felt. My arm was just dead, and the pain was intolerable. The last part of the season I was living on cortisone, Darvon, Excedrin and aspirin. I never had a day without pain, even when I wasn't pitching. On that day, though, Gibson pitched over his pain much better than I did.

Lolich really came on late in the season, winning his last four starts, and he was tremendous in the Series. He won the second game 8–1 and got the only home run of his career.

The Cardinals took the third game 7–3 because our pitcher, Earl Wilson, choked up. Earl's a great guy and I like him, but he had a habit of looking over his shoulder to see who was in the bullpen to save him when the game got around to the fifth or sixth inning. He simply had no guts in tough situations, and everybody knew it.

Gibson beat me again in the fourth game in Detroit. First off, the game should never have been played. It was raining cats and dogs but our stupid commissioner decided the viewing habits of 40 or 50 million television watchers were more important than the safety of the players themselves. It's a wonder no one was killed on that field. It was a quagmire and not safe even to walk on, much less play.

Regardless of the weather, I had absolutely no stuff. I couldn't have thrown a strike past my Aunt Maude. They cuffed me around and I was out of there in the third inning, got

0

dressed and left the clubhouse before the game was over. I thought the season was over. After all, St. Louis now had a 3–1 edge in games.

Lolich came through in game five, though, and we won it 5–3. Mickey gave up three quick runs in the first inning, but got himself together and blanked them the rest of the way. But the Cardinals should have won the game, and would have had Lou Brock slid into home in the fifth inning. Why he didn't slide will forever escape me, but he didn't, and Willie Horton threw him out.

Game six was back in St. Louis and I announced I was ready to pitch, if necessary. Dr. Russell Wright, one of our team doctors, had worked long and hard trying to rub the soreness out of my shoulder, and I had gone to Ford Hospital for a cortisone shot. I told Mayo I'd throw as hard as I could for as long as I could and that he should have someone heating up in the bullpen if I faltered at all.

I could have faltered and still won. Our guys got two runs in the second and ten (count 'em) in the third. It was a romp, 13–1. Northrup hit a grand slammer in the third and Kaline hit one out. I was plenty ticked off about losing my shutout. Roger Maris, Orlando Cepeda, and Julian Javier got singles in the ninth. The pitch Javier hit was a dandy. I had two strikes on him and I threw him a sidearm fast ball right on the fists. He blooped the ball just out of Dick McAuliffe's reach behind second base. It may sound selfish, but I really wanted that shutout, especially after the way I had pitched in my first two World Series starts.

Now comes game seven and Mayo asked me if I could pitch, if needed. I told him I'd do anything. He informed me I'd spend the day in the bullpen and be the first man in if Lolich got into trouble. Fortunately, Mickey never did.

He was tired, too, pitching with just two days' rest.

Nothing happened until the seventh inning when we had two on with two out. Northrup hit a drive to center field and Curt Flood simply blew it. Now, here's a super outfielder, but he just couldn't find the ball. He came in on the ball, realized it was over his head, and when he tried to back pedal, he lost his footing and the ball sailed way past him for a two-run triple. Freehan doubled Northrup home and we had a 3–0 lead. Don Wert drove in a ninth inning run to make it 4–0 going into the bottom of the ninth.

Mike Shannon hit one out off Lolich and Mayo went out to

talk with Mickey. God only knows what they said, but when Mayo got back to the dugout, he called to make sure I was ready. Had one more runner gotten on base, I'd have been in there. But Mickey got out of trouble and the World Series was ours.

We had champagne all over the place. It was the wildest scene imaginable. Then we continued to drink on the plane and I guess everybody in Detroit was matching the players, drink for drink. The entire downtown area was jammed, and there were so many people waiting to meet our plane they had to close the airport.

There were so many parties that night I only vaguely remember where I was and what I did.

The world seemed wonderfully warm, then. I had my beautiful wife, lovely children, a thirty-one-game season and the pennant and the World Series, big money deals in my pocket and the world by the ass.

Oh, really, Mr. McLain?

No, not really. But at the time, I thought so. Lots of people had Denny by the buns. It's just that in the thrill of the moment, I couldn't feel the pain.

Maybe it's like Jonah must have felt when he found himself in the belly of the big fish. Being swallowed up was a terrible thing, but he was alive and warm all over, and he must have thought, "Damn, I'm gonna get out of this mess after all!"

Jonah was luckier than I was. Or smarter. Or both.

FROM THE PENTHOUSE

2

TO THE SHITHOUSE

"It's just one step from the penthouse to the shithouse."

That's not an original quote by Dennis Dale McLain because I've heard it for years. But it's a beauty. Someone who has never taken that step can't possibly know how hard you fall. Let me tell you—it's more than just a little tumble.

As the people who call baseball our national pastime breathlessly awaited spring training 1970, I had everything anyone could possibly want.

I was not quite twenty-six years old. I had a beautiful wife and three lovely children. I was making at least $150,000 a year and maybe a lot more because I just couldn't keep track of things. By most folks' opinion (and sometimes my own, if pressured into the question) I was the finest pitcher in all baseball. Although I had a shoulder that was aching like hell 90 percent of the time, I knew in my heart that at any given time, I could retire any batter in the world, Killebrew or King Kong.

I had a successful night club act, a combo, a paint company, a flying service, I was getting into the organ business, land deals, sporting goods, and a game company. I had a house full of trophies, including two consecutive Cy Young Awards, Most Valuable Player, and a hundred more. Like I said, I had everything anyone could possibly want.

I had a lot more, too. They were things nobody in his right mind would want.

My wife, the FBI, the Internal Revenue Service, the commissioner of baseball, eighty-six creditors, and a few other vultures were on my back—all at the same time. On the outside, I was as happy as a whore in a lumber camp. Inside, I was dying.

I owed more than $446,000! At the time, I didn't even know what I had or what I owed. I just knew that the old line about "a fool and his money are soon invited places" fit me just fine. Giving me money was like putting perfume on a pig.

Now, I know what you're asking: How could a punk that age get into so much trouble? Damned if I know. I just kept digging a deeper and deeper hole and finally all these people just threw the dirt in on top of me.

Did I know all of that garbage would catch up with me someday? I suppose it's a lot like Richard Nixon and Bobby Baker and those guys with the pyramiding deals—you just never think it's going to happen to you. I kept thinking that somehow it would all work out. I knew no genie was about to pop out of a bottle and grant me three wishes, and I had no rich uncles to bail me out, either. But I somehow thought all the time, "This can't be happening to me." But it damn sure did.

My marriage was falling apart and it was 100 percent my fault. As for the money troubles, I've often said I place a lot of the blame on Arnold Palmer. After all, Arnie had the life-style I wanted. Matter of fact, he was the worst thing that ever happened to me. He was a great athlete, adored by millions, and counted his money like he counted his friends—in the millions. He flew his own jet plane around the country. He had business deals that made him even more money than his golf swing. Why wouldn't any kid want to be just like Arnie?

It made sense to me that winning thirty-one games one year and twenty-four the next, being named Most Valuable Player in the American League one season, and getting the Cy Young Award as the best pitcher in the American League two years in a row would be enough of a springboard to propel me into the land of eternal riches.

Every time I mention that I won the Cy Young thing two years in a row, someone always points out to me, "Don't forget, Denny, that you shared the Cy Young Award in 1969 with Mike Cuellar of the Baltimore Orioles."

Like hell I did. Mike Cuellar shared it with *me!*

I knew I wouldn't win it again in 1970. I knew it for a lot of reasons. For one thing, my arm was so pitiful there were mornings I couldn't raise a fork to feed my face. As it turned out, that's about all I would need my arm for that season.

When everyone else was gathering in Florida and Arizona to sweat off the pounds accumulated on the winter banquet circuit, I was sweating out my very future. While writers were speculating on whether I'd win twenty or twenty-five or thirty, I was wondering if I'd have a baseball in my hand except in the back yard with my kids.

My world exploded February 19, 1970, with this announcement from the office of Commissioner Bowie Kuhn:

> On February 19, 1970, I suspended Denny McLain from all organized baseball activities pending the completion of further investigation and my review of facts obtained therefrom. I based the initial suspension substantially upon certain admissions made candidly to me by McLain. These admissions related to his involvement in purported bookmaking activities in 1967 and his associations at that time.
>
> My investigation has continued since that date regarding McLain's activities and subsequent years. I am certain at this

0

time that my investigation has been thorough and has developed all pertinent information presently available. Pursuant to my powers under the Major League Agreement and Rules, I have now made the following findings and conclusions:

1 January 1967, McLain played an engagement at a bar in Flint, Michigan, and there became acquainted with certain gamblers said to be involved in a bookmaking operation. McLain at that time commenced basketball bets with this operation and subsequently he was persuaded to make financial contributions totaling approximately $5,700. While McLain believed he had become a partner in this operation and has so admitted to me in the presence of his personal attorney, it would appear that in fact he was the victim of a confidence scheme. I would thus conclude that McLain was never a partner and had no proprietary interest in the bookmaking operation.

The fair inference is that his own gullibility and avarice had permitted him to become a dupe of the gamblers with whom he associated. This, of course, does not remove the serious dereliction on McLain's part of associating with the Flint gamblers.

A thorough investigation has not revealed any other material facts beyond those I have described. There is no evidence to indicate that McLain ever bet on a baseball game involving the Detroit Tigers or any other team. There is no evidence to indicate that McLain gave less than his best effort at any time while performing for the Detroit Tigers. There is no evidence that McLain in 1967 or subsequently has been guilty of any misconduct involving baseball or the playing of baseball games.

McLain's association in 1967 with gamblers was contrary to his obligation as a professional baseball player to conform to high standards of personal conduct, and it is my judgment that his conduct was not in the best interest of baseball.

It therefore must be made the subject of discipline. In reaching my conclusions, consideration has been given to the fact that no evidence has been developed by my investigation that McLain's conduct apart from his 1967 associations has been inconsistent with his duties and obligations as a baseball player.

While it is true that in 1967 and subsequently McLain has been irresponsible in his personal financial affairs and that this is a source of serious concern, I have not in this particular case based my disciplinary action on such irresponsibility although the probationary aspects of my action are related thereto.

Under the circumstances it is my judgment that McLain's suspension should be continued to July 1, 1970. In the meantime his disassociation from all organized baseball activities must continue. In addition McLain will be placed on a probationary status and required to provide this office periodically with such data on his financial affairs as may be requested.

0

The purpose of this data is to satisfy this office that personal financial responsibility will not again contribute to leading McLain into such a situation as involved him in 1967.

Beautiful! Just beautiful?

Even with my limited schooling, I knew that "gullibility" meant stupidity and "avarice" meant greed.

I don't even remember the exact date I knew I was in *official* trouble. Hell, I knew I was in trouble financially, and I knew my arm hurt, and I knew my marriage was endangered, but I had no hint I was going to hear from the high priest of baseball. I guess it was about the second week in February when I got a call from one of my attorneys. He told me he had gotten a call from Jim Campbell, the general manager of the Tigers, who in turn had gotten the word from Bowie Kuhn that I was in deep shit.

Actually, I was suspended the very day I was to report to the Tiger camp in Lakeland, Florida. The actual letter from the commissioner was brief and to the point:

"This is to advise you that you are herewith suspended from all organized baseball activities pending the completion of the recently announced review which this office is conducting regarding certain of your personal activities. You and I have discussed today the reasons which required this action."

The shock of it all was so tremendous that to this day, I can't recall where I was when I got the call from lawyer Bill Aiken. I don't remember any of the conversation except that I had to fly with him to New York to see "the man." I don't even remember the plane ride there.

I don't know which was more agonizing, the period from February 19 to April 1 when I was waiting for Commissioner Kuhn to make up his mind, or the period from April 1 to July 1 when I finally returned to baseball. I guess it's like asking whether you'd rather be eaten alive by a shark or an alligator.

I was in the office of the commissioner, naturally, on that cold day in February when I got the news I was officially in trouble. I was at my home in Lakeland when I learned the extent of it. I recall at the time I was superhappy that it was only to last until midseason.

A lot of sportswriters, broadcasters, and some of my own teammates thought I got off with a slap on the wrist. Since most of the press had missed the crucifixion and only a handful were on hand for the massacre of Custer's people at Little Big

0

Horn, I could only surmise that they'd be happy only if Kuhn walked in with my head on a platter.

I imagine these sadists were delighted later in the 1970 season when I got hit with two more suspensions. In figuring out what I wanted to put into this book, I'll admit there were serious temptations to go into great detail about some of these sanctimonious writers and broadcasters who nitpick others while doing a considerable amount of gambling, drinking, and screwing around (not to mention taking gratuities and sometimes even money from the teams), but in the long run it might be better to see them suffer and wither away.

Don't get me wrong. I'm no choirboy, but neither are most of them! You open up most lives to the unending public scrutiny that mine has endured and you'll see a ton of flaws. It's just that the whole world knew about mine. The point is, the whole truth has never been told.

It began to dawn on me just before Christmas in 1969. I was in Viet Nam visiting our American servicemen when I got an urgent call from Sharyn. Now, here's a lady who really didn't know one helluva lot about what was going on behind the scenes. She knew I was moving pretty quickly and that I was into a lot of deals and that my life was one big rush. But she had kids to raise, and I simply didn't want to burden her with my troubles. I was still thinking at that stage that I could solve some and avoid the others.

I guess I was like a fighter who'd been taking a terrific pounding for about seven rounds, but was still on his feet. I figured I had a pretty good punch and might get lucky and score a knockout. As it turned out, you might call me the victim of a technical knockout.

Funny thing, the Federal Bureau of Investigation (those are the real, live G-men, folks) had come to me in November of 1968 after we had won the pennant and the World Series. It was right at the start of the Detroit auto show and I had a contract to appear there. I was having all sorts of pains in my right side and pretty much knew I had trouble with my appendix. But I didn't want to slow down long enough to have it checked, and figured I'd do it right after the auto show.

One Friday morning I got a call from Jim Campbell and he told me to get my fanny down to Tiger Stadium because two guys from the FBI wanted to talk with me. Let me tell you, that was a mighty long ride from my house in the suburbs down to the stadium.

0

Jim introduced me to these two fellows, then just the three of us went into the offices of John Fetzer, who owned the Tigers. Campbell wasn't involved in the meeting. They were nice guys and they asked me lots of questions about my associations and so forth. They asked me if I gambled, and I told them yes. They never asked me if I was involved in a bookie joint.

Now, I really don't think I lied to those gentlemen. It's just that I did not tell the complete truth. I figured they really didn't have anything on me and probably were after bigger fish, so why should I implicate myself any more than I had to? Anyway, I wasn't represented by an attorney at the meeting and I had trouble figuring out just what they were driving at. I never heard another word from the FBI until January of 1970.

During the 1969 season it popped into my mind every so often, but by and large I figured it had pretty much blown over. As it turned out, 1969 was like a hurricane sitting around waiting to build up strength. In early 1970 it was a raging storm that practically destroyed my life.

The FBI contacted me again right after I had gotten back from Viet Nam, and we must have met six or seven times. There were two other tie-ins to all this. *Sports Illustrated* magazine was preparing a story about me and it became apparent the magazine had given Commissioner Kuhn advance details.

Too, there was a massive gambling raid on New Year's Day in 1970, one of those cross-country things that involved long-distance phone calls. The late Dizzy Dean was wrapped up in that betting scheme, but got off because he cooperated with the government. So—as they say downtown—the heat was on.

I had been on the cover of *Sports Illustrated* before, but on those occasions it had been pleasant. This time, in the issue dated February 23, 1970, my glowering face was accompanied by two headlines that said, "Denny McLain and the Mob," and "Baseball's Big Scandal."

There is some truth in the story. About 10 percent of it. The rest is a pack of lies and I should have sued *SI* at the time, but I was talked out of it, though to this day I don't understand why. The caption on the main picture accompanying the text of the story described me as "poor, dumb Denny McLain." I guess I couldn't argue with that, because I was about to be poor and I can't deny that I was dumb at the time. Still, the magazine is guilty of libel and defamation of character and any jury in the land would uphold my side in a suit.

0

I *was* involved in a bookmaking operation, or at least I thought I was. I had become entangled, or perhaps engulfed is a more appropriate word, in 1967. A Flint radio broadcaster named Pete Sark had gotten me an engagement to play the organ in a Flint steakhouse called the Shorthorn. I think I got $500 a week.

We started playing there in 1967, in October, just after we had gotten nosed out for the pennant. The manager of the Shorthorn was Clyde Roberts and he seemed like a nice enough fellow. He bet on all sorts of sports and he'd tell me about his bets and so forth, and finally I began to bet with him, maybe $20 or $30 a bet. I won some and I lost some, nothing serious.

We drew lots of people on that engagement so they asked us back in January. Clyde and I were betting college and pro basketball and, as they say in the trade, we weren't exactly breaking the bank. It was costing me $200 or $300 a week, so finally Clyde said to me one day:

"Why should we keep losing our money like this? I know some guys who bet pretty good, and we could go into the *other* end of this business."

I'd been around betting all my life, but actually I didn't grasp what he meant at the time. So Clyde, kind soul that he was, laid it all out for me—how we'd become partners in a bookmaking operation, how we'd never take anything more than a $100 bet, how we'd make certain that all bets had to be cleared with me, and how we'd make a fortune. It all sounded pretty attractive to me, but I wanted to check it out with a good friend of mine in Detroit.

Now, by this time I had met two other fellows who were to become involved in this tragedy. One, Jiggs Gazell, I met just once. He was to be our partner. Another fellow, named Johnson, was either a bookie or a runner for one.

I rushed back to my home in the Detroit suburbs and had a summit meeting with Ed Schober. Ed was an executive with Pepsi Cola and he liked me because I drank gallons of the stuff every day long before I was successful enough to be asked to endorse it. Ed and I had become good friends and, with our wives, spent a great deal of time together.

I put the deal on the table for Ed, and he bought it as eagerly as I had. He didn't know any more about this type of operation than I, and both of us expressed concern that there

0

would be Mafia involvement. Clyde assured us we'd operate quietly and on a small scale with no mob interference.

Here was the deal: Clyde and Jiggs were to run the operation for 50 percent of the profits, but if we lost, Schober and I would have to pay everything. Frankly, I didn't see how we could lose. All we needed was a few customers who were as lousy at handicapping as myself. I went to a bank in Flint and borrowed $4,000 to get the operation started. After all, you have to have a bankroll if you're gonna be a bookie.

Right off the bat, we started on a losing streak and I had to go back to the bank for another loan, about $3,000 as I recall. I figured it was just a mild cold snap and we'd make a quick recovery. Soon afterward, I left for spring training in Florida, confident our little scheme would put extra dollars in my pockets. It never happened.

The bookie operation didn't really get rolling until late spring or summer, but I was betting during spring training. Clyde was mailing me the betting sheets and like an idiot I didn't make much of an attempt to hide them. I even used the pay telephone in the Tiger clubhouse to call in some bets long distance.

Sometime during spring training General Manager Jim Campbell, Manager Mayo Smith, and Rick Ferrell, Campbell's assistant, called me into the office and asked if I was doing any betting. I wasn't totally truthful with them. I told them I made an occasional bet, but that it was nothing serious.

It really wasn't, until one Saturday afternoon in August. As I recall, I had pitched and won that day. That evening, Schober called and said, "Denny, we just got hit for forty thousand dollars."

I don't even remember what I said, or what I did, but I knew right off something was fishy. First off, there was an agreement we were not to take any big bets, and any bet of any consequence had to be cleared with Ed or me. No one cleared anything that day.

When Ed talked with Clyde and Jiggs, they identified the "lucky" bettor as one Ed Voshen. Now, I had not met Ed Voshen then, and never met him since. As it turned out, Voshen reportedly was a pretty heavy gambler. He owned a truck stop near Battle Creek, Michigan.

According to *Sports Illustrated,* Voshen tried to collect his winnings from Jiggs, then from Schober, then from my father-

0

in-law, Lou Boudreau. The magazine went on to say that when Voshen got nowhere with any of them, he then turned to the Mafia and finally got an audience with Anthony Giacalone, reputedly one of the top Mafia people in Detroit.

The story went on to say that a gangland court was convened in Giacalone's boat well on the Detroit River and that another gangland meeting was held at Hillcrest Country Club in Mount Clements, Michigan; and that after first declining to get involved, Giacalone decided to get the thing settled.

There then was supposed to have been another session at the boat well, with me ordered to appear in front of Tony and his brother Vito (Billy Jack) Giacalone. According to the story, the brothers Giacalone went into a rage, demanded that I come up with the money to pay Voshen, and just to make certain I understood them, Tony brought his heel down on my toes.

Garbage. All of it.

To this day, I have never met either of the Giacalone brothers and have never been in any boat well on the Detroit River and the only people who ever brought their heels down on my toes were batters trying to beat me to first base when I was covering the bag.

Sports Illustrated was guilty of the worst kind of character assassination and tried to tie me in with other so-called Mafia or Cosa Nostra types. It said we finally came up with more than $40,000 for Voshen, but that Voshen never got the money; and that it wound up, for the most part, in Tony Giacalone's pockets.

Voshen was killed in a car wreck in mid-October of 1968, and I still hadn't met him. He was supposed to have bet several thousand dollars on a horse named Williamston Kid the previous September at the Detroit Race Course.

If indeed he did bet that kind of money with Jiggs or Clyde—and I don't think he did—then Clyde and Jiggs had no business taking that big a bet without consulting with myself or Ed Schober. If he didn't, then some folks tried to set me up for a big killing.

I got out of the bookie business the day that big bet was to have been made. Now, up to that time, I'll admit I played the role of the big dealer. I had a telephone in my car and I even made some bets on that phone. You just can't get any dumber than that, because those phone calls can be heard by anyone else who has a car phone. I even had a second phone installed in my house in suburban Detroit and went so far as to put it in-

0

side a desk. At the time, I thought of myself as being a pretty good-sized wheeler-dealer. I also thought I was going to get rich at this little scheme.

After the big "hit" that Saturday, we started getting the pressure. First, there were calls from Clyde Roberts to Schober, and Ed then would relay the information to me. Frankly, Ed and I panicked pretty quickly.

Before long, Ed got a call from a fellow who said his name was McCann and he made his point pretty clear. He told Ed he was acting in Voshen's behalf and that if I wanted to avoid some embarrassment, I'd better cough up the money.

Finally, arrangements were made for me to meet Voshen. I wanted to explain my side of the deal to him, to tell him that the bet hadn't been authorized, and that I couldn't come up with the money. I was en route to Chicago and was to meet with Voshen in Battle Creek. He never showed, and so I called his office and was told he was out of town.

Later on, a meeting was arranged at a restaurant called Topinka's Country House on the northwest side of Detroit. I waited for an hour, and Voshen never showed.

Meanwhile, Schober kept getting threatening phone calls from McCann, who finally told him he, meaning McCann, had won a lot of money from Voshen in a gin rummy game, and Voshen had told him to get the money from us. He said he had Voshen's note and didn't intend to get stuck with it.

One day, a man identifying himself as Voshen called Lou Boudreau, told Lou of my involvement, and threatened to go to baseball officials if I didn't produce the money. Naturally, I had to come clean with Lou and tell him of my involvement. Lou took the phone call as an attempt at blackmail and reported the incident to the FBI. He never heard another word from anybody.

Schober and McCann decided on a twenty-cents-on-the-dollar payoff, and Ed and I came up with several thousand dollars, using money we had gotten in a loan from the Citizens Commercial and Savings Bank in Flint.

Apparently that satisfied McCann enough to take some of the pressure off us.

And I was out of the bookmaking business. I wasn't worried about some clown killing my wife and kids, and it never occurred to me that all these things would come back to haunt me and deprive me of making a living.

As I look back, it's nothing short of a miracle that I was

able to concentrate enough to have the kinds of years I had in 1968 and 1969.

There's one more thing involved in all this. When we were getting the greatest pressure—during the 1967 season—I was told that the "big man" behind the whole scene was a restaurant owner in Flint. I don't know whether it was bravery, or stupidity on my part, but I drove up to see him. I didn't tell anyone where I was going. In fact, I told Sharyn I had to go to a banquet.

I walked right into his private office and there he sat behind a desk. He was a swarthy guy and he seemed surprised when I confronted him. If he knew who I was, he didn't let on. I seem to recall he said something like, "Can I help you with something?"

All the way driving up to Flint, a distance of about forty-five miles, I had been rehearsing my little speech. I was going to be brief, blunt, and brave. I was going to tell him that I thought I had been duped, that the deal was for all bets to be cleared through me or Schober, that I thought we had been set up, and that all these phone calls from Voshen or McCann or whoever were part of a master plan to shake down a couple of dummies, and that I heard he was behind the whole thing and that I wanted to know the truth.

For the life of me, I can't remember exactly what I did say when I finally got in front of him. I remember starting out by saying, "My name is Denny McLain."

Big deal! It's a wonder I could remember that much as scared as I was.

I tried to explain the situation and when I finally ground to a stumbling halt, the guy just looked at me and said something like, "So, what's all this supposed to mean to me?"

He told me he never heard of any bookmaking operation, never heard of my involvement in it, didn't know anybody by the name of Ed Voshen, had no interest in any of it, and couldn't care less if I bet, paid, or welshed. It was pretty obvious we had nothing further to discuss, so I left.

I was never so glad to get out of any place in my life. I wanted to run to my car but that would have been too obvious. I did walk at an accelerated pace.

Today, I can laugh about it, but there was nothing funny about it at the time. When I got into my car, I recall putting it into reverse to back out of the parking stall. When I applied my foot to the brake pedal before turning out onto the highway, my

0

right leg was shaking so much I couldn't get going. I was jumping up and down so much inside that car I felt I had a thousand Mexican jumping beans crawling around my body.

I don't know how fast I got back to Detroit, but if A. J. Foyt was on the highway that night, I'm sure I passed him. And all the time I kept looking into my rear view mirror, fearful that some Mafia goon was coming after me to run me off the highway.

By the time the gambling thing blew wide open early in 1970, I had a thousand other problems. I was living each day as if it would be my last, and it's a wonder each day wasn't.

When my lawyers first started questioning me about the bookmaking and the gambling, I denied everything. Finally one of the attorneys spoke up:

"Listen, son, they've got the dope on you. They know everything you've done and when you did it. We can't represent you unless you come clean and tell us the truth. When they start telling us things we don't know about, we can't even come up with a reasonable answer. So the truth has to come out, and you might as well start now."

So I told them everything, then began to cooperate fully with the government.

All this came on the heels of that New Year's Day raid (which is beginning to sound like the Valentine Day's Massacre), and the activity was unbelievable. Schober was scared out of his wits and so was I, but all the time the government people were nice to us.

Meanwhile, Commissioner Kuhn's own investigation was being headed up by Henry Fitzgibbon, a former FBI agent. Charles Segar, then the secretary-treasurer of baseball, also was involved. Incidentally, Segar treated me like the scum of the earth.

Jim Ritchie was heading up the government's Organized Crime Division Task Force in Detroit. The U.S. attorney for Southeastern Michigan was Jim Brickley, who later was to become lieutenant governor of the state. Both were very nice to me and I'm sure they know I was taken down the road by some pretty sharp hustlers.

I appeared voluntarily before a federal grand jury and so did Schober. We had four or five meetings with FBI agents. I had a handful of attorneys going out of their skulls. Bill Carpenter from the McCormack office was trying to unravel me from a personal management standpoint; Bill and Bob Aikens

0

were handling the corporate liability stuff; Fred Walker was our criminal attorney and Archie Katcher was waiting in the wings, ready to handle our bankruptcy stuff. Little did Archie know how much work he had in front of him, nor how quickly he'd have to get at it.

One day after our appearance before that federal grand jury in Detroit, we were summoned to the office of the commissioner in New York.

Three of us made the trip—Aikens, Carpenter, and myself. We met briefly in the McCormack offices in the General Motors Building, then went directly to the commissioner's office. Our first meeting with him lasted no more than twenty minutes. He asked me a series of questions and I answered them candidly. He then told us to wait in an outer office.

So we waited for the longest two and one-half hours in the memory of mankind! Finally he called Aikens and Carpenter back into his office and gave them the bad news—an indefinite suspension.

The two attorneys came out of Kuhn's office and I stood up. As it happened, I was standing near a window. Carpenter spoke, and as I try to reconstruct the exact scene, it seems he said something about there being both good news and bad news. He asked which I wanted first. I told him to tell me the good.

"Well, we don't know how long 'indefinite' means."

I wanted to know what the hell he meant by that. So I told him to hit me with the bad news. It was then that he told me the commissioner had placed me under indefinite suspension.

I turned to the window and put my hands on the sill. All the blood was rushing out of my system and I felt weak. The sweat was pouring out of me and I could feel myself trembling.

I wanted to jump right out of that damned window. And I looked down, ten or twelve stories or whatever it was, to the streets of New York below. There, walking, was a group of Boy Scouts.

"Just my luck," I figured. "Sure as hell, I'll jump and smash into them. I'll probably kill half a dozen of them, but they'll break my fall then some asshole will arrest me for negligent homicide."

When we left the office, Jerry Green, a sportswriter for the *Detroit News,* confronted us. He had been hounding us all day. Moments later, we faced a sea of writers and broadcasters. I don't even remember what I said, but it wasn't much. I was shell-shocked. We took a private elevator down to the street, and sure enough, there was Jerry on that elevator. I grabbed a cab and headed for the airport. Again, there was Jerry and he asked if he could ride to the airport with me.

"Sure, if you pay the cab fare."

So the two of us went to John F. Kennedy Airport where I caught a flight to Tampa, Florida. I was living in nearby Lakeland at the time and all I wanted to do was get back to my family.

I'll say this for Jerry: He was doing his job well. I've been tremendously upset at some of the things he has written. But that day, we were like Siamese twins.

The plane ride to Florida was weird. I was traveling under the name of Mr. Arthur and I was seated beside an elderly man. He asked me my name and I blurted out "McGrath." He asked what I did, and I told him I was an airplane pilot specializing in crop dusting. All the way back we talked about aviation.

When the plane touched down in Tampa, I still had a forty-five-minute ride to my home, but before that I had to face what appeared to be thousands of people asking me questions and shoving microphones in my face. I tried not to say much of anything, surely nothing that would get me into any more trouble. After all, at that stage of the game, I didn't know whether I'd ever pitch again.

Little did I know then that the commissioner of baseball was gutless. He couldn't find a fire if he were surrounded by smoke. He calls me into his office and sits me down and tells me he understands how a young fellow could get drawn into a lot of bad deals with all the pressures and everything, then he lowers the boom on me.

I can't say it any better than Marvin Miller, the executive director of the Players' Association, did: "McLain is the victim of self-incrimination. Bowie called him into his office for an informal discussion and said, in the manner of a forgiving Dutch uncle, 'Tell me all about it, Denny.' Then Denny speaks, and discovers he has incriminated himself."

All right, here I was in Lakeland, just moments from where my team was starting spring training. I not only couldn't play baseball with them, I couldn't even associate with them. So I played golf. And I mean I played it—more than most of the touring pros.

0

All during spring training, Bowie Kuhn, who hadn't been commissioner very long, was making the big tour of the camps. He'd send word in advance that he wasn't about to discuss my situation. He was getting ripped pretty good, too, by the press. He started out being a vague and pompous commissioner, and if nothing else he's been consistent.

Perhaps the first person who knew exactly what the commissioner had decided to do was former President Nixon. On the last day in March, the commissioner made the annual trip to the White House to give the President his baseball pass and Nixon asked Kuhn if he'd made his decision on Denny McLain. Kuhn told the President he had decided to suspend me until July 1, 1970, and the commissioner later quoted Nixon as saying the judgment was a fair one.

It really warms the cockles of my heart to know that Richard Milhous Nixon approved of my punishment. Too bad Spiro Agnew wasn't a pitcher.

The following day, the commissioner announced his decision to the world. I was out until July 1. I began fidgeting and Kuhn began squirming. Right away someone asked him the difference between intending to be a bookie and really being one, and would you believe the commissioner said it was like the difference between murder and attempted murder?

The reaction was divided. Many writers and fans felt I had gotten off with a simple wrist-slapping. Others felt that since I had not been convicted of anything, except in the commissioner's kangaroo court, I ought to get off entirely. I had mixed feelings myself. Ninety days was a long time, but it wasn't the end of the world.

So I missed the Detroit Tigers' first seventy-one games of the season. The way I look at it, I missed twenty starts and God knows how many victories and how much money.

I had been making $90,000 a year from baseball and a ton on the outside. Problem was, I had been spending two tons for each ton I made.

If I listed all the claims against me, this book would be thicker than *War and Peace*. The rent hadn't been paid on my home and the owner was suing me for $2,450. A former secretary wanted $209. Uncle Sam was pressing me for $9,460 in back income taxes. A utility company was suing for $807. The owner of a flying service wanted $10,000. The claim from an airport we used amounted to something over $600.

0

The Michigan Securities and Exchange Commission was looking into our paint company, Denny McLain Dyco International, accusing us of a violation of the blue sky laws—selling stock before we had been incorporated.

We had a handful of companies—the international company; Denny McLain Dyco Paints; Denny McLain Jet Travel, a charter airline service; Denny McLain Associates; and Denny McLain Enterprises, Inc., and some other involvements that I can't even recall.

Okay, I was being tossed out of baseball and my house at the same time. My whole world was coming apart, and there wasn't a thing in the world I could do about it.

I had to begin a mad scramble for money. At the time I still thought I could bail myself out of my financial jackpot. The night I was suspended I flew to Detroit, did a television show, and hurried right back to Florida. I then did a TV bit with Joe Garagiola and picked up a quick $1,000. I went to Canada on a personal appearance. I had some offers to play semi-pro baseball in Ohio and Iowa. There were night club offers from Los Angeles, Toronto, Las Vegas, and some other places (at the time I didn't think Vegas was conducive to a reform), and I had offers to write a book.

I thought about going to Japan to play baseball, but once you've played in the big leagues, and you're still young enough to play there, anything else is strictly second class.

Besides, ninety days wasn't all that long, and after all, hadn't I just turned twenty-six when I was suspended in the spring of 1970? I wasn't even nearing my prime yet! How many guys are through at that age?

Before I could get back to baseball, I was busted. I mean bankrupt, kaput, it's all over and done with. I not only didn't have a pot, I didn't even have a window to throw it out of.

Good old Denny. Never does anything halfway.

I owed $446,069.96. My assets, all put together in one little pile, amounted to $413.00. One of my attorneys described the situation beautifully. Bill Aikens, after filing the bankruptcy petition for me, called it "a straightforward proceeding because there simply isn't anything."

I didn't have to be told that, but it was shocking nevertheless.

Try this on for size: In the two years prior to my financial collapse, I had made a total of more than a quarter of a million dollars. I filed for bankruptcy in early June of 1970—and the previous September I owed nothing more than some $10,000 to the government for back income taxes.

Here I am, nine months later, owing nearly half a million bucks!

Last year, the Detroit Wheels of the World Football League fizzled out to the tune of $2.5 million in a matter of months and that's an overwhelming amount of mismanagement; but remember, they had a *team* going for them in their failure.

I did it with the help of just one other person. His name is Edward May.

I call Ed the "Houdini of the legal profession" and it's a good thing I can laugh about it now or I'd break his neck. Matter of fact, he's not in the legal profession any longer and the only thing he can cause to disappear is himself. But when I knew him (and I really didn't know him until it was too late) he could make money disappear right in front of your eyes. Strangely, it was always someone else's money.

Leave it to me to get hooked up with an attorney who'd later be disbarred for misuse of clients' funds.

I met Ed May through one of my old teammates, Joe Sparma. Ed was so charming he not only had Joe into some deals, but Al Kaline as well, and I knew Al had always been very careful with his money.

In July of 1969 I put every single one of my business affairs into Ed May's hands. I had gotten into the Dyco Paint Company in spring training of that year, and we had so many other things going I simply didn't have time even to write a check for my telephone bill.

Ed May was going to save me all that trouble.

He'd take my money, including the paychecks I was getting from the Detroit Tigers, and do wondrous things with it. What a magician he was!

The deal was this: Ed May had the power of attorney, he was to write the checks for everything including my house payments, utility bills, all of it. All I had to do was make it. He was my personal manager, my attorney, counselor, overseer—hell, he was running my life, it was as simple as that.

I'll say this for Ed, he talked big. No sooner had we joined up than he suggested we build or buy our own plant in the Detroit area and manufacture the Dyco paint ourselves. We had been doing just fine as a distributor, but that wasn't big

O

enough. Why should we pay top dollar and be nothing more than a distributor? Why not put the stuff out ourselves, and cut out the middle man? We'll make three times as much money, right? Right? Wrong, wrong, and wrong some more! We lost our ass.

Maybe it was like monopoly to him. Certainly, I didn't have the time to handle the financial end of things, and Ed May didn't have the brains or the character to handle things for me.

I'm not trying to win any popularity contest, never have and never will, but maybe I am looking for some type of understanding as to how this sort of thing could happen.

I was a punk kid of just twenty-five when I hooked up with Ed May, when all these tremendous things were happening to me. I'm no Rhodes scholar now, but I was a lot dumber then, and a lot more impressionable. He was a fast talker and he impressed me as a guy who was eager and aggressive and who could get things done. And that's precisely what I needed because at that stage of my life I simply didn't have time to do things myself.

The first thing Ed wanted to do was to get rid of all the people around me, the people I had been doing business with, the people I had some degree of confidence in—all of them! He said they were parasites who were feeding off my success.

It was like a lion shooing all the flies away so the lion could have the carcass all to himself—and Edward May was the king of the beasts!

Like I said, the only thing I really owed back then was some money for back income taxes. I had payments to make, like everybody else, but the only honest-to-goodness debt was to the Internal Revenue Service. We had to get an advance on my salary from the Tigers to pay for that. So we met with Jim Campbell and as I recall we got $30,000.

As we left Jim's office, the last thing Campbell said to us was this: "Now, before you guys do another thing, write that check for the back income taxes."

Jim and I have had harsh words from time to time, but then, and now, I'm persuaded that he's always had my very best interests at heart.

So we left the office, Ed May with the $30,000 and me brimming with confidence that my finances were in good hands.

Uncle Sam never got a dime!

0

The government later grabbed my furnishings and personal possessions—sold them at auction for $5,582 and applied that against taxes I owed for 1968.

So now it's June, I'm not pitching baseball, I have no airline company, no paint company, no fat contract with an organ company, no one beating down my doors to sign rich contracts and play the big night clubs, and not a dime to call my own. I owe everything from $6.75 to Orange County, California, to $160,000 for the collapse of the paint company.

Even Ed May listed himself as one of my creditors, to the tune of $23,500!

I had fired him during the winter after finding out how deep a hole he had dug for me.

Even after I filed for bankruptcy and got out from under all those debts, there were other holes that kept opening up, and I kept falling right into them. I confess I had a hand in digging every one of them.

While sweating out my suspension, I stuck around Florida most of the time, and I stuck by the rules and regulations Commissioner Kuhn had set up for me. And I was in pretty good shape, or in as good a shape as you can be when you're not in actual game competition.

I played golf, and I did a lot of throwing and some running, although I confess I'm not as fond of running as, say, Jim Ryun. Or Ma Perkins.

There had been a tremendous amount of publicity about my return. I was to pitch July 1, 1970, and the crowd of 53,863 was the biggest in Tiger Stadium since 1961. It was a sweltering night in Detroit, muggy and ninety-one degrees, and I managed to hang around for five and one-third innings. I didn't have much. I gave up eight hits including three home runs and left without being involved in the decision.

Seventy-one writers covered the game. I knew what to expect from them, but the reaction of the fans surprised me. I'd had my troubles with them from the start, but they were phenomenal to me.

My pitching was pretty sloppy in the next few weeks. I had four lousy starts, then won a couple with relief help. I finally found myself in my thirteenth start and for the first time since coming back, went all the way for a victory. It was my third victory of the season, and as it turned out, it was my last.

Don't ask me what made me do what I did. I was just full of hell, and I did it. It's as simple as that.

0

It was August 28 of that year and we had a night game against Oakland. About an hour before the game, I pulled off a stunt that was to get me in trouble again.

The newspapers had been all over me about my ineffectiveness, and I was fed up with the writers. They just didn't seem to grasp any of my side of the story. It was cut and dried, win or lose. It was as if I was letting *them* down, instead of myself and my family and my teammates.

I had come to the park late in the afternoon and all of a sudden I had a brainstorm and I relayed my plot to pitcher Joe Niekro, whose locker was next to mine. "Let's get those fucking writers," is what I said. Joe liked not only my idea but my way of expressing it. I conceived the brilliant notion of throwing water on a couple of them.

It was a childish prank and I admit it. It also was a very expensive one, but at the time I had no idea it would be taken so seriously. Now, we didn't have any particular writers in mind. It was blind luck. If you came into the locker room first, you got a bucket of water on your body. Nothing complicated about that, right?

The plan was this: Joe would engage a writer in some conversation, and I'd do the dousing. First writer in was Jim Hawkins of the *Detroit Free Press.*

I already had two buckets of water in my locker. I got warm water from the whirlpool bath, then put towels over the buckets to hide their contents. It was about quarter to six when Hawkins came over and we started talking about sportswriters. He was facing Joe, answering a question, when I got him. I poured a whole bucket right on top of his head.

Funniest thing about it was that Hawkins never moved. He just stood there. Finally he took off his coat and put it over a chair in front of a fan, so it would dry. Hawkins went to the john to straighten himself around, and soon as he did that, Niekro sprayed talcum powder and epsom salts into the fan. When Hawkins came out, his coat was a legitimate mess.

Normally, we have six or eight writers parading through the clubhouse before a game, but this was really an off night. Even though we had the trap all set for another sucker, not a single writer came in. So we went out, had infield practice and everything, and finally about seven thirty or so, I was back in the clubhouse.

In comes Watson Spoelstra, who then was covering the Tigers for the *Detroit News.* Now, Waddy, as he was known,

was a hell raiser of the first order in his younger days. He even cut another sportswriter's tie off one night; and sped off in his car and left a friend stranded when the guy got out to pee on an expressway.

In Waddy's later years, though, he became rather drab and humorless.

When he came into the clubhouse, he strode right to my locker and said someone had told him I wanted to see him.

Well, right then I knew someone had given him the message just to set him up. We talked for a minute or two, and when he turned to walk away, I couldn't resist so I threw another bucket of water on him.

The plan was for all the players in the clubhouse to stand and applaud when I got him with the water. Well, when it happened, only Tom Timmerman clapped, and I think he gave it just one little clap. No one said a word, including Spoelstra. He quietly took off his coat and walked out of the room.

When he was gone, the whole locker room exploded in laughter.

It was funny only until the first inning. I was sitting in the dugout beside Manager Mayo Smith and when the phone rang I picked it up. It was Campbell.

"Dennis," he barked, "you come up to my office as soon as the ball game is over."

It seemed like the game would never end, but when it did I marched my little fanny right up to Campbell's office. In the meeting besides Campbell were Mayo and Rick Ferrell.

Campbell: "Did you throw water on Jim Hawkins and Watson Spoelstra?"

McLain: "No."

Campbell (incredulously): "You didn't?"

McLain: "No, I didn't throw it. I dumped it."

Christ, but Jim was boiling. What little bit of hair he had seemed to be standing on end. He was glaring at me when he announced, "I've got no alternative except to give you an indefinite suspension."

I think for a minute or so I actually cracked up mentally, and lost complete control of myself. If Jim hadn't been all the way across that big desk of his, I know damn well I would have hit him. I was that hot.

I got down on my knees in front of all of them and I remember I was yelling and screaming at the top of my lungs, begging to be traded. I was bellowing at Campbell, telling him he was horseshit and that the town was horseshit and the fans were horseshit, and all I wanted now was out.

When I got through with my tantrum, I barged out of his office and slammed the door as hard as I could. I don't know whether I broke it or not, but if the thing didn't break, it'll last forever.

Once I reached the parking lot, some of the other players had finished dressing and were going to their cars. I remember that Bill Freehan and Don Wert and Dick McAuliffe were there, and I told them I had been suspended. Just about that time Campbell came by and he was still in a rage.

Freehan isn't my favorite person of all time, but he walked toward Campbell to try and intervene. Jim brushed everybody aside, saying, "I oughta suspend all you bastards."

Well, a general manager is tough enough to deal with, but a pissed-off general manager is impossible. The following day several players met with Jim in his office and the word was they were going to try and work things out. Forget it. The suspension sticks.

Campbell had told me to apologize to the writers, and I did. Both of them were tremendous. Hawkins, in fact, said he took the whole thing as a joke and that no apology was necessary.

Spoelstra had called Campbell just minutes after I doused him, but he was super when I talked with him. He actually broke down and cried on the telephone, because he's a guy who has known some personal grief in his time. It really was one of the most touching conversations I've ever had with anybody, and after we hung up I thought there was a real chance the whole thing might blow over. It never did. So I went to Florida to rejoin my wife and kids.

By this time, I had become associated with the Mark McCormack people in Cleveland and they were trying to untangle my affairs. The fellow working closest with me was Bill Carpenter.

The word was out that my suspension was to be for seven days; thus it was to end on September 5. The day before it concluded, though, we got word that the commissioner wanted us to come to New York for another meeting.

Carpenter gave me the bad news and said the commissioner's office wanted to talk with me about my carrying a gun. The club was going to New York anyway for a series beginning on September 9 so the commissioner ordered the Tigers not to reinstate me until after our next summit meeting.

0

It was a two-hour session and looked for all the world like a meeting of the United Nations General Assembly. The way things went, I was the only foreigner there, though. With me were my attorneys, Carpenter and Aiken. Also on hand were Campbell, Smith, and Farm Director Hoot Evers from the Tigers. The commissioner, the high priest, presided, naturally, and with him were attorney Paul Porter, security chief Henry Fitzgibbon, and my good friend Mr. Segar.

Commissioner Kuhn allowed as how my behavior was "not consistent with his probationary status." The bill of particulars, according to the commissioner's information, was that I had displayed a pistol in a Chicago restaurant, that I threatened a parking attendant in California, that I regularly carried a gun, and then of course there was the incident with the writers and the buckets of water.

We learned quickly that one of my Detroit Tiger teammates was supposed to have ratted on me for carrying a gun. It was one of my old battery mates, catcher Jim Price.

The truth of the matter is that for a long time, I had owned not just one gun, but several guns. I had a .38-caliber revolver, a rifle, a .22 pistol, and several other guns. As for displaying a gun in a Chicago restaurant, that never happened.

As for threatening a parking lot attendant in California, I had a shouting match with an attendant at Anaheim Stadium who thought I was going to park in Gene Autry's space. But there was no gun-toting there, and not a single threat. Now the commissioner's right-hand man, Joe Reichler, told me Jim Price was coming in to testify against me.

Price never showed, and Fitzgibbon, who conducted the investigation for the commissioner, said he never heard that anyone was going to do any such thing.

Price is the guy who wanted to buy a gun because he had been robbed earlier that year. I told him about my revolver and he asked me to bring it on our next road trip. So I did. The only time I brought it out of my suitcase was in a hotel room in Milwaukee and there were three of us in the room at the time. A friend of Jim's from Chicago had brought in another gun to show Jim, and I don't even remember what kind of weapon it was.

Whatever kind it was, it went off in that room. Either Jim Price or his buddy fired it. I never fired my gun, which incidentally I had obtained from a relative of mine on the Chicago

0

police force, and which I had registered with the proper authorities in Michigan.

I'll confess I didn't have a permit to carry a concealed weapon, but thousands of people in Detroit carry guns. After all, Detroit is Murder City and getting bloodier every year. Besides, the city had just experienced a terrible race riot when I decided to keep the gun around.

I didn't wear it on my hip, but I did keep it in my car most of the time. I often carried large sums of money (although never enough, it seems), and I had received threats from time to time. Sharyn had been scared half to death when some clown put a smoke bomb in her car. So, yes, I owned a gun, and I sometimes had it with me because I feared for my own safety and well-being and that of my family.

The bottom line out of the meeting was that they wanted me to dispose of my guns, which I agreed to do, and they wanted me to go to a head-shrinker. It was more of an order than a request, so I agreed to go to a psychiatrist.

I couldn't get out of that office fast enough. It seemed that every visit there cost me something more out of my life. I was afraid next time they'd pack me in ice and ship me to some mortuary.

An interesting sidelight is the cab ride I had to the airport. The driver started talking about how 75 percent of all the taxi drivers in New York carry guns for their own safety and he was hopping mad because baseball was trying to kick some poor slob pitcher in the ass for carrying one.

I told the cabbie I was in total agreement with his point of view. Trouble was, he wasn't commissioner.

The real one got word to me that there was to be still another meeting—at the tail end of the season—at the airport hotel in Newark, New Jersey. Kuhn and another of his coolies showed up, asked me the same tired questions, got the same tired answers, then asked me if I'd like to be traded away from Detroit.

At this stage of my life, I'd have accepted a trade to play for Duncan's Restaurant pickup team in the Sunday morning Central Park league.

Kuhn told me it'd be Washington, D.C.

It was a trade engineered by the commissioner of baseball, and one that required him to be devious enough to circumvent his own rules.

O

I was under suspension, you see? And a player under suspension cannot be traded. So, Kuhn informed the press, he had secretly lifted my suspension on the last day of the regular season, so the Tigers and the Senators could approve a deal the commissioner had devised.

At the time of the trade, I was sane if not sound.

Sane? You're damned right. In a two-page report to Commissioner Kuhn himself, the psychiatrist said that good old Denny "is not mentally ill and not in need of such service."

That's one of the nicest things ever said about me, especially in 1970!

The visits to the psychiatrist were things of beauty. The whole thing was arranged through the doctors at Ford Hospital in Detroit.

It's one thing to go to a psychiatrist or psychologist when you're feeling low and down and out and you want to find out something about yourself. That's *voluntary!* It's a whole different ball game when you're *ordered* to go. I mean, you go there half-thinking you're a little crazy.

I don't even recall how many visits I had with this guy, maybe three or four, but there's one I'll never forget.

The psychiatrist was a strange dude with a German accent. He talked like one of those storm troopers in a World War II movie. He wore a white outfit that didn't come close to fitting him. Hell, it wouldn't have fit Smiley Burnette.

First thing out of the box, he takes me into a sterile room. Man, I mean sterile. There was one chair and one table in the room. No windows. No pictures. No television set, no radio, no books, no magazine, no nothing.

The good doctor, who might have been a consultant for the Luftwaffe at one time or another, then gave me a present. It was a puzzle. A big, plastic puzzle. Naturally, it wasn't put together. Denny McLain never gets anything the easy way. The frigging thing was in a zillion pieces. Well, maybe thirty or forty.

Somehow I knew that down deep inside me I had quickly formed two dislikes, one for the good doctor, and one for that puzzle of his. I'm just not fond of puzzles. It's as simple as that.

"Relax, Mr. McLain," he ordered. "Just relax and see if you can work the puzzle. It's really very simple."

Nothing, but nothing is very simple for Dennis Dale McLain. If, by chance, something is simple, I complicate it.

Herr Whoever-He-Was left the room and told me he'd be back shortly.

0

I'll be damned if I was going to work that puzzle. Kid stuff, I figured. So I sat. And I sat. And I sat. There just wasn't anything else to do.

I thought briefly about playing with myself, but sure as hell the doctor would have been looking through a secret window in the ceiling.

Out of sheer boredom I turned to this idiotic puzzle. Any clown can work a puzzle, right? Besides, the pieces were pretty good-sized. I tackled it, much like a mouse would attack a cat, and with approximately the same degree of success.

I'll be damned! I could not work the thing. It just wouldn't fit. I thought maybe it was like my life—try as I might, the pieces just would not go together. I don't have what you'd call the longest fuse in the world, and in a mild fit of pique I took my arm and swiped the whole thing off the table and onto the floor.

Just about that time Dr. Gobbledegook strolled back into my cell. He looked down over his glasses at the puzzle strewn all over the floor, then he looked at me.

"Excellent, Mr. McLain. Excellent."

I couldn't believe my ears. He thought I did very well. And they think *I'm* crazy!

THE MAKING

3

OF A PITCHER

From the time I was twelve or thirteen years old, I dreamed of making the big leagues. I think every kid who ever played the game dreams of that. For me to say that I knew, or even sensed, that I could make it would be one of the biggest lies I've ever told—and I've told a couple or three in my time.

I jumped the first club I ever made—setting the pattern for the kind of situations that were to follow. My father started me playing baseball when I was six. The Little League minimum age was eight but some folks started a team in Midlothian, Illinois, about ten miles from where we lived in Markham. I remember the tryouts were at the ridiculous hour of eight in the morning. I was a couple of years younger than most of the kids trying out, but I made the team. Then never played a single game. They were serious about their baseball then, and they had workouts three or four times a week; and I simply couldn't get to and from the practices.

Later that same year my dad started his own team with a couple of his friends. We really didn't have a very good team, but it was good experience and the competition was fierce.

The league was called Boys' League and my dad was president of it until he died. By that time they had gotten a Little League franchise from Little League headquarters in Williamsport, Pennsylvania.

When that happened, though, I was playing Babe Ruth League baseball. I had to cheat to get in that, too. I played for a team in Harvey, about ten miles from our town. Since we had no team in Markham, I had to come up with a fake address in Harvey.

The year my father died, we won the state championship in Babe Ruth and went to Ypsilanti, just outside of Detroit, to play in the regional championships. I pitched the first game and won it 2–0. We lost the second game 1–0 and I made the error that let in the only run of the game. It was not one of my better days. I made the last out, too. I just stood there like an idiot and took three fast balls right down the pipe. Just couldn't pull the trigger.

We had won the state championship in Harvey—and that's where I met Sharyn.

I had unofficially lost my amateur status long before I started getting a reputation as a good high school athlete. The firemen's club in Markham had been paying me five bucks a night to play softball, and I had sold myself to play for a Pony League team for gasoline money and a little something extra.

0

But that lasted only a couple of games, because the fellow who made the deal with me didn't come through with the money as he had promised.

In high school I was no honor student, but I had no time for bookwork. Sports was all-consuming for me. I played junior varsity football for a few weeks, long enough to score a touchdown the first time I carried the football, and long enough to learn I didn't enjoy getting belted around. My dad and my baseball coach weren't too keen on me playing football anyway.

I didn't burn anything up my sophomore year in high school. Playing basketball, I suddenly made the discovery I couldn't see the numbers on the uniforms. That's when I started wearing glasses.

We won everything at Mount Carmel High School. In my four years of baseball there, we won the City League championship three times. Our coach, Father Austin, was a beautiful man. He taught and talked baseball fifty-two weeks a year. I think he hated all other sports and all other coaches.

In my junior year I led the city in just about everything—pitching, hitting, and home runs. Shortstop was my main position and I loved it because you were always in the middle of the game. I did some catching, too.

My father discouraged me from throwing a curve ball. He said I had to wait until my arm was fully developed and that if I tinkered around with breaking stuff in high school it'd hurt my arm.

We were going to play St. Rita on the day my father died—it was May 4, 1959. Naturally he was coming to see me pitch. He died right in front of Comiskey Park. I've always felt, down deep, that that was the reason I finally decided to sign with the Chicago White Sox. I felt I was supposed to—even though I was more of a Cubs' fan when I was growing up. Signing with the White Sox just seemed like the right thing to do.

I could have signed with several clubs. The Yankees made an attractive offer and the Phillies did, too. Funny thing, the team I really wanted to play for—the Cubs—never even nibbled. You suppose they knew I'd be burned out at age twenty-six?

The deal with the White Sox wasn't all that lucrative. The total package was $17,500—ten thousand for signing, and the rest in contingency bonuses based on my progress. The money was gone pretty quickly because I bought a car for my mother and one for myself.

The toughest thing, I mean the absolutely toughest thing,

about signing a professional baseball contract was facing the inevitable fact that I was not going to be able to see my girl friend every night. I was in what you might call a state of enchantment. I thought at the time she was the only girl in the world, and there was no way I wanted to play baseball somewhere else, with her sitting back in Chicago.

But Harlan, Kentucky, beckoned. My career was calling. I was gone.

It was my first plane ride. We took a two-engine job to Knoxville and then a bus to Harlan to play in the Appalachian Rookie League. I checked into the only downtown hotel. There, Cecil Perkins, my first roommate, and I examined the contents. Two beds. A sink. No bathroom. But it was professional baseball and, by God, I was a part of it. So nothing else really mattered. Except I missed my girl back in Chicago.

My manager was Ira Hutchinson but we were together for only two games. In that brief time, he tried to teach me how to throw a curve, but quickly gave up. I just couldn't do it. At that time, I really didn't need it.

My professional baseball debut came on the night of June 28, 1962, against Salem. I had super smoke. It was quite a debut. I struck out sixteen and didn't allow a hit and won the game 9–0. Next time out I struck out sixteen more, but lost the game on an error. I was on my way.

Next stop: Clinton, Iowa.

The hitters in the Midwest League were unimpressed with the credentials I brought with me from Harlan. I struck out ninety-three batters in ninety-one innings, but lost seven of eleven decisions.

After that season, the White Sox sent me to winter ball in Sarasota, Florida. There, Bruce Howard and I became good friends. As it turned out, he was to play a major role in my career.

The White Sox had invested a considerable amount of money in Bruce and in Dave DeBusschere. The following spring, everyone knew they couldn't keep all of us. Someone would have to be left unprotected in the draft.

In spring training of 1963, Bruce and I were to face each other in a squad game. Everyone knew that the loser was gone. I lost 2–1, even though I struck out eight or ten. The next day I was gone, drafted by the Detroit Tigers.

It turned out to be the biggest break I ever had!

DeBusschere was going to be kept around because the

club had invested about $75,000 in him. Howard stuck because he had a pretty fair slider. I was gone because I had a straight fast ball. Nothing else. The White Sox manager at the time was Al Lopez and he was known as an excellent handler of pitchers. He worked hard with me to try to get some spin on the ball to make it curve, but I just couldn't do it.

I later learned the Tigers had been scouting me for a whole year. Everyone knows about everybody else's players, and the Tigers were aware of the fact that the White Sox couldn't protect all three of their young pitchers.

So on April 8, 1963, I became the property of the Detroit organization. The Tigers sent a man to Sarasota to escort me to the Tigers' minor league headquarters at an old army air corps base just outside Lakeland, Florida. The place was not anything at all like the Essex House or the Continental Plaza, but I guess in all fairness the young players there weren't performing like major leaguers, either.

I was assigned to the Duluth-Superior team in the Northern League and we ran away with all the marbles. Our manager was Bobby Mavis and he quickly saw the futility of trying to teach me anything about a curve ball. In that league, I didn't need anything but a fast ball. Jim Rooker, who later was to make it with the Pirates as a pitcher, was playing the outfield and he was knocking down the fences. I was winning everything in sight, so by the time I got my record up to 13–2 I was promoted to Knoxville in the Sally League. Everywhere I pitched, I was striking out a lot of batters and walking very few, but the victories were harder to come by in Knoxville.

In my first appearance, I got my brains beat out. The first two innings against Chattanooga were cake. I struck out five of the first six batters and didn't give up a hit. In the third inning they hit some shots that nearly tore the paint off the walls. I was ready to quit.

Romance was on my mind again. Sharyn Boudreau and I had been dating since January, I was spending a fortune on long-distance phone calls and the batters realized, as I did, that I was a one-pitch pitcher. Besides, I had my music. I played the organ, and since the age of fourteen had my own rock group.

Despite my mediocre record at Knoxville, the Tigers called me up to the major leagues in September. I was just nineteen. The club was in Washington when I got orders to report. I couldn't get there fast enough.

General Manager Jim Campbell was on the same plane, although I didn't know him at the time. He introduced himself and when we got to Washington he even paid the cab fare. We went directly to the ball park. It was a Friday evening and the Tigers and Senators were playing a twi-night doubleheader. I think we got there during the first game.

It was a dream come true, but I wouldn't permit myself the luxury of thinking I was there to save the franchise. I had sense enough to know I was just getting the once-over. After all, I had won eighteen games in the minor leagues—using just one pitch.

Someone gave me a uniform and I went to the bullpen and spent the rest of the first game just staring. There were only three or four thousand people in RFK Stadium, but when you've been playing in front of six hundred they seemed like a ton of folks. I couldn't get over the lights, how bright they were. In some minor league parks, the lights are so bad in the outfield you chase fly balls by the sound of the ball rotating in the air.

Every time I looked up, there was an airplane in the sky. I finally started counting them and got up to 164 before my neck gave out.

One of my unfavorite people of all time, Hank Aguirre, lost both ends of the doubleheader that night, as I recall. He got the crap kicked out of him as a starter in the first game. Our manager, Charlie Dressen, had told Hank to keep the ball away from Jim King. Hank gave him one of his infamous screwballs and King hit it nine miles.

Then in the second game, Charlie was looking for somebody to get one batter out in the ninth inning. Hank was about 16–14 at this time and naturally wanted all the work he could get to try to win twenty. He volunteered and Charlie put him in to face Jim King again. Same pitch. Same lousy pitch. King hit this one ten miles.

When a rookie comes to a major league club like I did, the veteran players normally don't put down a red carpet for him. Let's face it, there's a chance he might be taking one of their jobs. So the relationship, especially between a rookie pitcher and veteran pitchers, tends to be a bit strained.

Rocky Colavito was most friendly to me, even offered me his warm-up jacket to use in the bullpen. Al Kaline came over and said hello. Gus Triandos was one of the catchers and I talked briefly with him. Dressen just said hello the first night, but the following day sat me down for a little chat. He said he

0

wanted to start working with my curve ball. I explained, "Mr. Dressen, we will have to start from page one."

"Hang loose," Charlie said. "You'll be doing some pitching for me, but I don't know when. But just be loose."

I tried to be cool and loose but I was scared. My roommate was Larry Foster. He was a straight-arrow guy—never drank and never swore. So every day we went to the park, got something to eat after the game and went home to bed. I was in awe of everything and everybody. Especially Dressen. I immediately liked him. After all, he's the guy who called me up to the major leagues. And he had a reputation of liking overhand pitchers, and that was Dennis Dale, full out.

The first full day he took me to the bullpen and worked twenty or twenty-five minutes with me. On that very first day, he taught me how to spin the ball properly, so at least I had a bit of a curve ball. I was no Sandy Koufax, but at least I had the threat of a curve.

It was Chuck Dressen who convinced me that with a great deal of work, I could possibly someday be a pitcher instead of just a thrower.

Curiously enough, the pitcher whose place I eventually took on the Detroit Tiger roster helped me, too. After having won a couple of games for the big club at the tail end of the 1963 season, everyone—myself included—assumed I'd be with the major league club all of 1964. In spring training, though, I was short of phenomenal and they sent me to Syracuse to start the season. I was about ready to quit then, too, except that Dressen had told me I simply needed some regular work, and that if I did well at all, I'd be back with the Tigers.

Frank Lary, the old Yankee-killer, had given me some pretty good pointers in spring training. Here was a guy with, very candidly, a minimum amount of what we call "stuff." His fast ball was okay, his curve ball acceptable, and his change-up decent. He messed around with a couple of other pitchers once in a while, too, but Frank was not overpowering in any way. He had tremendous courage, and a lot of pitching know-how, and he won a bunch of games because of those things.

It was ironic that when the Tigers called me up from Syracuse in late May of 1964, Lary was sold to the New York Mets to make room for me on the roster. Casey Stengel was managing the Mets then, and it was no wonder he took a chance on Frank, even though his arm was bothering him. Lary used to eat the Yankees alive when he was at his best.

O

But, back to when I first came up to the majors.

Dressen worked with me, and talked with me every day. He had told me on a Thursday, I believe, that I would get my first major league start on Saturday afternoon, September 21, 1963. I didn't sleep for two days. It's tough to sleep when you're sitting on the crapper all the time.

Bill Freehan warmed me up before the game but Gus Triandos caught the game. I guess Charlie wanted the more experienced guy in there with a raw pitcher. Mike Hershberger was the first batter I faced in the majors and I walked him on four pitches. Then I picked him off first.

The next batter might have been Don Buford. I remember he gave me trouble all day and got three of the seven hits I gave up. I think he got on by a walk, too, then damned if I didn't pick him off, too.

Charlie Dressen is screaming in the dugout, "For Christ's sake, you guys can't pick anybody off base and here's a nineteen-year-old kid and he's picked off two in one inning!"

What Charlie didn't know was that Hershberger and Buford were the first two base runners I ever picked off in my life. I was so high mentally that day that the juices were racing through me every which way, and I guess that made me much quicker than normal.

I also got my first home run of my professional career that day. Fritz Ackley, a right-hander, was the Chicago White Sox starter, and I know the fact I was pitching against the team that let me go made me higher, too.

In the fifth inning, Fritz fed me a high fast ball and I hit it into the left field stands. I don't even remember my feet hitting the ground on the trip around the bases. I recall looking up at the clock and it was 2:22 in the afternoon. Billy Bruton hit one right after me to give us a 3–1 lead, but I managed to blow that with a wild throw that let in a couple of runs in the eighth. Then Norm Cash hit one out off Jim Brosnam to win it for me in the eighth.

I was almost in a coma in the ninth inning.

First man up was Deacon Jones and he flied to Rocky Colavito in right. A tough hitter, Pete Ward, was next. I got two strikes on him with fast balls and damned if Triandos didn't call for a curve ball. I had thrown only two of them all afternoon and neither was in the strike zone. But I was certain Gus knew more about the situation than I did, so I did the best I could. It

0

was a hanger, a little high, but Pete took it for strike three. He must have been too shocked to swing. Then I got Charley Maxwell on fast balls for my eighth strikeout and my first major league victory.

No one in my family saw my major league debut. I later learned that my Uncle Jack McLain walked into my aunt's home in Grand Rapids, Michigan, and found her crying, listening to the Tiger–White Sox game on the radio. She was my dad's sister, and she knew how much he had dreamed of his son someday being a major league pitcher. That day, I became one.

Next time out I got creamed by the Washington Senators. I wasn't around long enough to break a sweat but I remember Dressen telling me to keep the ball down. Hell, I'm a high fast ball pitcher and I hadn't purposely thrown two balls down in my entire career. Don Zimmer hit one nine miles and somebody else cleared the fences and I was out of there.

I got to pitch the last game of the season against Baltimore. We beat them 7–3 although Jim Gentile hit one of my watermelon fast balls into the stands, nearly breaking the back off a seat. I struck out eleven, but the thing that made me happiest was seeing Charlie Dressen's quotes in the newspaper the next day. The Tigers had finished in a fifth-place tie with Cleveland and lost more games than we won, but Dressen was asked what had pleased him most about the season and he said, "The kid who pitched the last game and the kid who played right field."

Willie Horton had played right field, had three hits including a home run in the season finale, and batted .326 in the last three weeks of the season. Charlie would never live to see the Tigers get all the marbles, but he could sense they were on the way back.

If you'll check it out, you'll find that the last game of the season most often is a quick one. Let's face it, in ninety-nine instances out of a hundred the season is over and the players are anxious to get packing and get home. On that final day of the 1963 season, Wally Bunker and I made it longer than the Normandy invasion. It was Wally's first major league start, and he wasn't too sharp. As for me, I took every batter to a three-and-two count and threw about 175 pitches. It was not one of my more artistic efforts.

Every time I looked up, I had runners on base. The Orioles

got ten hits and I walked eleven more. It looked more like a track meet than a baseball game, but winning is what counts. The affair lasted nearly three hours.

A few days later, Sharyn and I eloped to New Buffalo, Michigan, and got married by a justice of the peace. Then I headed for winter ball in Dunedin, Florida, to perfect my other skills.

Dressen had said publicly, and he had told me, that he was counting on me to be his fourth starter in 1964. His instructions for winter ball and spring training were simple: "Just look halfway decent."

That's just about what I was—halfway decent. All I did in spring training was to go through the motions and prepare myself physically. In the first spring training game against the Minnesota Twins Dressen sent me out in relief and I didn't get anybody out. Finally I worked with the "B" squad and I got the shit kicked out of me there, too. Right before the big club broke camp to head north, I got the news I was being farmed out to Syracuse. I wanted to die.

The Syracuse club opened the season in Jacksonville and then went to Atlanta. Sharyn went on to Syracuse to look for a place to live. I went back to Lakeland to get our car, then drove all the way to Syracuse. I nearly had a terrible wreck on the way north and I was in a horrible frame of mind. I was going to do so well in the major leagues, and here I was heading back to the minors and wondering if I'd ever really make it.

As it turned out, I pitched just eight games for Syracuse. I had won three out of four decisions; we had moved into a small apartment and bought furniture when Tiger scout Frank Skaff came out of the stands and informed me I was heading for Detroit.

It was no great shakes in Detroit, because I was hurt much of the time. I pitched in only nineteen games and worked a hundred innings, losing five out of nine. I never really felt strong until our trainer, Jack Homel, finally rubbed the soreness out of my shoulder in late August.

That winter, most of the Tigers' young players who were destined to lead them out of the wilderness went to Mayaguez, Puerto Rico, for a season of winter ball. My marriage was great; I won sixteen and lost only two and got along beautifully with Manager Bob Swift; someone stole my wallet with $400 in it; we got ripped off buying jewelry at least half a dozen times; and we learned to dig foxholes in the bottom of the team bus

0

when unruly Puerto Rican fans started attacking our bus after games.

The night we won the playoffs the opposing fans were so riled up they started rocking our bus and broke every window in it.

The American players were making a thousand dollars a month, but some of us struck a private deal with Babel Perez, the president of our club. He was a super guy with a dandy-looking daughter whom we didn't dare look at—besides, I was newly married and couldn't have cared less. As I recall, there were three of us who had a side deal with him. I was in on it and so was Joe Sparma, and it seems there was someone else. The deal was this: If we won the first playoffs, he was to give us an extra thousand dollars each. When we won, we went to collect our bonus but he wouldn't pay us. We threatened not to play in the championships, but chickened out.

But professional athletes are whores when it comes to money. You perform, and you're paid. I know my heart wasn't in it when we played the championship, and if your heart isn't in it, there's no way you can perform at your best.

I know I learned a great deal in Puerto Rico because I was getting a steady diet of pretty good hitters, some of them major leaguers. I struck out Orlando Cepeda four times in a row, and he was quoted as saying he thought I should win twenty games the next season.

I won sixteen, but at the same time I lost only six.

By 1965 I was a much better pitcher, though certainly not a finished product. Dressen had me working on a change-up and the curve ball was improving.

If I could point to the one game that turned my confidence around it would be the night I pitched in relief against the Boston Red Sox. It was the night of June 15, 1965. Dave Wickersham had started and the Red Sox drove him out of there and Dressen put me into the game in the first inning.

He made the move so quickly I only had time for about twenty warm-up pitches, but still I fanned Ed Bressoud and Bob Tillman to get out of further trouble in the first inning. Then I struck out Earl Wilson, Lennie Green, and Dalton Jones in the second.

In the third, I got Carl Yastrzemski and Felix Mantilla, and had a string of seven strikeouts in a row, a major league record for relief pitchers. The record would have been eight except that umpire John Rice blew a call. I had Lee Thomas in the palm of my hand with two strikes on him and threw him a letter-perfect curve ball. It was the only curve I threw, so the only thing I can figure is that Rice was so surprised to see McLain throwing a curve that he automatically called it a ball. The next pitch was a low fast ball and Thomas grounded out to second base.

That night I wound up with fourteen strikeouts in six and two-thirds innings, and from that night on I knew I could pitch, and win, in the big leagues.

It's a funny game—the following year I didn't pitch nearly as well as I had in 1965, yet I won twenty games.

You hear lots of talk about pitchers trying for the corners and pitching to spots. Through all of the early part of my career, the only spot I pitched to was home plate. Through 1965 I was basically a fast ball pitcher. By 1966 I had a fast ball, a dinky curve ball, and a straight change-up. In 1967, under the influence of pitching coach Johnny Sain, I began to experiment with a lot of sidearm stuff and tried to throw the slider. At first, I resented him because I thought he was trying to force a pitch on me, and it was a pitch I had a great deal of difficulty mastering. Most guys pick up the slider real well, but it took me a year to do it.

Dressen hated the pitch. He said it was too much strain on the arm unless thrown perfectly, and that certainly wasn't the way I was throwing it. By 1968 Sain convinced me that the only way I would ever learn to throw the slider was by going out there and throwing it, making mistakes with it, and hoping that through a lot of hard work it would come to me. Damned if it didn't.

About the fifth or sixth start of the season, it started working. I started throwing it hard and it had a great downward motion to it.

I was never what you'd call an overpowering pitcher, but the slider gave me a whole lot more ammunition. I had great command of the pitch and could throw it for strikes any time I needed it. It was a great "out" pitch for me, and I've always felt confidence was as much a part of pitching as "stuff."

When I had all those pitches—and confidence in them—I became a legitimate major league pitcher. And I was learning things about hitters, too. I realized then that all hitters can be jammed, no matter how good they are. And I realized that all the really good hitters can handle a ball away from them.

0

Surviving the 1966 season was a major chore. Dressen, who had been ill during part of 1965, died early in 1966, and Bob Swift, who had been acting manager before, became the manager. Cancer finally got the best of him, and we wound up with Frank Skaff as our manager.

There was a whole new regime in 1967. Mayo Smith became the manager and brought Sain in as his pitching coach.

I'm going to do a whole chapter on managers I've loved, hated, and endured later on, but my early feeling about Mayo was horseshit. Here, I had won twenty games and he's making statements that made me feel like I had to win my job back all over again.

In spring training I started off slowly and then tailed off. I couldn't get my grandma out, and things didn't get a whole lot better once the season began.

Of course, by that time I was involved in a lot of other activities that took up my time and I'm sure much of my thinking. Then there was the foot injury and the hassle with Mayo late in the season, when I could have won twenty and the Tigers could have won the pennant. It was a year I'd just as soon forget, in a hundred different ways.

Even if sometimes I didn't perform like a full-fledged major league pitcher, I at least knew I was one. I also was discovering, by this time, that I was not only a major league sucker, but an Olympic one.

But, then again, nobody's perfect.

TEAMMATES I HAVE KNOWN
(AND LOVED AND HATED)

4

Baseball produces strong friendships and strong hatreds because from February or March until October you are in a confined atmosphere that closes out almost everything else in your life. You stay at the same hotel, eat in the same restaurants, dress in the same locker rooms, ride the same buses and airplanes, and then go out and play games together—on the field and off it. I started to say that baseball players sleep together, but we'll amend that to say that they sleep in the same room, presumably in different beds.

It's impossible for twenty-five players to spend that much time together and not have differences, even raging fights and arguments. I don't buy much of that "togetherness" bullshit that a happy team is a winning team. The Oakland Athletics of recent vintage are the greatest argument against that.

It is my opinion, though, that if a team has a manager the players like, or at least can tolerate, it makes for a better team. Our 1969 Detroit team was publicly accused of lying down like a bunch of dogs, of being quitters. There's no question that our morale was down, and I'm sure there were times late in the season when we were disgruntled, and down mentally—all of which results in sub-par performances.

Late in my career, I spent some time with the Oakland club and although there were differences and disruptions, most of them are traceable to the owner, Charlie Finley. He has to be the biggest clown the game has ever known, but I'm convinced it is Finley who keeps the club together. The players have such a common bond in their collective hatred for the man that this hatred makes the A's an even better team when they cross the white lines. And they are a supremely talented group of athletes.

The Tigers weren't, when I joined them. We had a wild mixture of players, half of whom were too old and the other half too young. But we grew, somehow, into a world championship team, the younger players developing in time to dovetail with the last hurrahs of the veterans.

When you're young and you come up to a major league club, you're automatically in awe of those who are already there. If you're nineteen, as I was, you're in awe of everything and everybody. Here I was, about to pitch to Mickey Mantle, a player I had idolized since childhood. Anyone not in awe in that situation has to be a complete, babbling idiot or worse.

As a kid, I loved the Chicago Cubs and my favorite pitcher

was Bob Rush. I also had a great liking for Phil Cavaretta.

In high school, I followed all the major league box scores and naturally saw some games on television. I wasn't so long removed from that hero-worship stage when I found myself in a major league uniform. The realization that these people are human, too, that they take baths, become parents, pay bills, laugh and cry like anyone else hadn't hit me yet.

At times, it seems to me, it never really hits the writers and the fans.

Probably the one player who was exactly as I thought he would be was Al Kaline. It didn't surprise me, either, when Al decided to call it quits in 1973. Most truly great athletes know better than anyone else when the time has come to hang them up. Al has been a quality performer on and off the field and he'd have made twice as much money had he played either in New York or Los Angeles. I think the Tigers always thought Kaline should be a big leader and all that, but Al's just not the type, never has been and never could have been a leader. He leads by example, but he's simply no holler guy.

Now, the main holler guy with the Tigers was Bill Freehan. Freehan's a great competitor and very knowledgeable as a catcher. After 1966 I think Bill knew as much about the game as anyone in the league. But there were things that worked against Bill.

He came out of the University of Michigan and no one could question his brains.

But what the Tigers needed more than brains was an arm, and God didn't give Bill Freehan a very good one. When he threw to second base, they should have invoked the infield fly rule. Runners have stolen the Tigers blind for years and they always will as long as Freehan is catching, unless they come up with a designated thrower rule.

When Freehan joined the Tigers he had this "two-four-six-eight, who-do-we-appreciate" attitude. Maybe that's part of the Big Ten syndrome, I don't know, because the only syndrome I'd know about would be the Mount Carmel High School variety. Freehan's a rah-rah guy and he tried to instill that in the Detroit clubhouse.

No way, pally. It just won't work. You simply can't get up for every game, because you're doing it day in and day out, a hundred and sixty-two times every year. It's not like pointing for the big football game a few Saturdays each fall. I don't think

Freehan ever understood that. He's a nice guy, though, who tried to please everybody; and I doubt that he ever walked onto a field without the feeling that he could win.

And he had what our guys used to call the "Big Ten trot" and we used to make fun of it. I think down deep inside himself, Freehan always hoped he'd become the leader of the Tigers, but it never happened.

Funny, he wanted to lead and couldn't, and Kaline should have been a leader but refused to be. It's unfortunate that a man with that much ability didn't take charge, but I suppose it's because he's basically an introvert. Still, I maintain that Kaline should have been a centerfielder from the very start of his career. He didn't want any part of it, though, and no one ever stood up and ordered him to play there. But Al had enough class to keep silent when he didn't like someone, and like all of us, he liked some managers better than others.

The two strongest men I ever met in baseball were Frank Howard and Willie Horton. I think someone said it first about Harmon Killebrew, but it applies just as well to Howard and Horton, that they could hit a baseball out of any park in America, including Yellowstone.

We were with the Knoxville club in 1963, and I witnessed an amazing feat of strength on the part of Horton. We were playing in Lynchburg, Virginia, when Willie lost his temper. It could have been his life because let's face it—in 1963 you should not be black, and be in trouble, in Lynchburg.

The opposing pitcher threw a fast ball behind Willie's head and before Willie could get the bat out of the way, the ball hit the bat and went straight up into the air to the pitcher. The pitcher caught the ball, then stood there laughing his ass off. Willie took about ten steps toward the dugout, then made a beeline for the mound. I swear, if he had gotten to the pitcher he would have killed him.

It had been a bad night for us from the very beginning. I had been tossed out in the first inning for arguing, and another pitcher, Fritz Fisher, had been ejected, too. So all of us were a little short-tempered, but Willie took the prize.

The umpires threw Willie out, of course, and he headed for the clubhouse in a mighty rage. The door was locked and someone ran to get the key, but Willie wanted in the clubhouse, and he wanted in right that instant. Damned if he didn't put his hands on either side of that door and break the chain link fence and lock. I made up my mind right then and there that if Willie

0

and I ever got into any kind of hassle, he would be declared the winner by forfeit.

Willie's major problem is that he gets so damned much advice and listens to all of it. And he's been babied for years in Detroit.

If Willie Horton had been born white, the Tigers would have dumped him years ago. But he was born practically in the shadows of Tiger Stadium, was a high school hero and still lives there, and he's the main player the black fans have identified with over the years. The Tiger front office used to be accused of having a quota for black players. It may have been true years ago; I don't think there's any substance to it now. But Horton has been pampered beyond belief, and as a result, Willie has pampered himself.

It's also true that Willie has been victimized by people in the black community. Willie didn't have the educational opportunities that many players have had, so he's naturally been more gullible. The hustlers know that, and they've always been in Willie's life. Generally speaking, the person whose advice Willie heeds is the last person to talk to him. I mean, if God himself came along and was first in line, and Randolph Ripoff was last, then Randolph Ripoff got the deal, and Willie got screwed.

When he first came to the Tigers, Willie looked like a truck trying to catch fly balls in the outfield. But he worked his fanny off and became an acceptable fielder.

As for hitting, there never has been any question about his abilities.

Charlie Dressen got more out of Willie than anyone else. That's because Charlie understood Willie.

I'm not sure how much formal education Charlie Dressen had, but he was a master psychologist. He knew Willie had to be pampered, but Dressen did it the right way. He told Willie repeatedly how important he was to the club.

And I'll give Mayo Smith a lot of credit for the proper handling of Willie in 1968, when he won the pennant. Willie played 146 games that year, more than he's ever played in the big leagues, and was a major factor in our winning it all.

He's the one who won my thirtieth game for me, against Oakland, and I've always loved Willie. But I'd be willing to bet he'll wind up busted, because of the people around him who'll constantly take advantage of him. And the minute he's washed up, these same people will drop Willie like a bad habit.

0

Willie's always been a pretty trusting guy, and as a result he's been easy to con.

It may be difficult for an outsider to believe, but the Tigers used to buy Willie's checks and gift certificates from him at drastically reduced rates. It's not uncommon for players to get checks of twenty-five or fifty bucks, or gift certificates for the same amounts, for appearing on postgame or so-called star of the game shows around the league. Because Willie swung a pretty good bat, he'd get on these shows quite frequently.

On long road trips, most players figure out ways to run short of money. It always seemed Willie was one of the first to get the "shorts." When he was low on cash, it'd be bargain time—in the clubhouse, in hotel rooms, on planes.

"Okay, gents, I have in my hand a gift certificate for a fifty-dollar pair of shoes," Willie'd shout. "What am I bid?"

One of the cheapies always started the bidding at some ridiculously low figure of five dollars, and sometimes it wouldn't get much higher than that. Everyone would be tapped out on the West Coast trips, and we tried to buy Willie's gift certificates with checks, but Willie hated checks and wouldn't take them. Matter of fact, when he got checks for appearing on radio or television shows, he'd sell the checks. The man simply hated checks, and I often thought maybe Willie figured they weren't as good as money.

One time Gates Brown bought a pretty good radio from Willie for three dollars. The bidding started at two dollars and Willie was screaming, "Man, I can't go nowhere on a little bitty amount like two dollars. Let's get serious about this bidding."

Three dollars was as serious as anyone got, so Willie sold the damned thing. It must have been worth ten times that much.

I've always thought of myself as being a pretty prejudiced individual. Someone once said that until the day comes when you could accept the thought of your child marrying someone of another race, then you're prejudiced. If that's the case, then I'm loaded with the stuff. I mean to tell you, I don't want to guess who's coming to dinner. I damned well want to know.

But I grew up with blacks and went to school with blacks and competed with and against blacks and have socialized with blacks all my life.

Now, if I were asked to name the player I've had the most fun with during my entire baseball career it'd be Gates Brown,

0

and there's never been any question about Gates being black. Here's a guy who served time in the Mansfield (Ohio) Reformatory, and he not only paid his debt and his dues but he's been willing and able to talk about it in such a way as to help lots of other people.

Gates and I always kidded each other about this racial thing. I always lived in a lily-white suburb of Detroit and Gates would kid me about coming over to my house for dinner.

"Why don't you come over Saturday night?" I'd ask him. "But make sure to come in the back door, and wear a white outfit so my neighbors will think you're coming to cater the meal or clean the carpet."

Gates would inevitably respond by calling me a flock of names. His favorites were "white pig" or "honky." Perhaps some liberal whites and militant blacks could never understand the special relationship Gates and I have enjoyed over the years, but that's their problem and not ours.

I've been asked if openness and candor like that, and that type of joking around would help ease racial tensions and bring about more understanding between the races. The answer is probably not, because there are too many people who have hatred buried down deep inside them, people of both races who really don't want to end the struggle. But in a one-to-one situation, people can find a solution that works for them and I had that kind of relationship with Gates, and to a lesser extent with Willie Horton and Jake Wood and many other black athletes I've known down through the years.

It's a great injustice that Gates Brown hasn't been permitted to play more. The rap against him was that he was a liability with the glove. No question about it, Gates would never get a Golden Glove award, but he could have been acceptable had he been given a chance to play more frequently. But that sort of thing happens all too often in baseball, a guy getting tagged with the reputation of being a butcher in the field, then largely being ignored as a fielder rather than having someone work with him with an eye toward gradual improvement.

If someone hadn't worked with Horton, or with Jim Northrup for that matter, they'd have been relegated to the bench on a permanent basis. A routine fly ball was a thrilling adventure for the team and the fans when Northrup first broke into pro ball. And he later became a pretty fair man with the glove.

0

But of all the baseball players I've ever known, I'd have to rate Jim Northrup as the one I like least. Maybe I'd put him in a dead heat with Mickey Lolich, but no worse than that.

Northrup truly is the most selfish athlete I've ever known. He cared about no one but himself, but sometimes you can get by with that in a game like baseball, and Northrup proved that point through many seasons.

If we won a game and Northrup didn't get a hit, he'd be absolutely miserable in the clubhouse. He'd snarl at everyone and everything. Believe me, this happened for years. His entire composure and attitude depended strictly on how he performed as an individual. On the other hand, if we got the bejesus kicked out of us and Jim had a couple of hits, he'd be the happiest player in captivity. I think Jim Northrup must have been pissed off when he crawled out of the womb and he's never changed. I don't know how Jim treats his wife and kids, but I'd bet he kicks hell out of stray dogs.

When he hit one out or got a couple of hits, it never seemed to matter that his team might have lost the game. And when he didn't get a hit, he'd call the pitchers every rotten name in the book. "Motherfucker" was always a popular favorite of Northrup's and he'd save it for the opposing pitchers or the umpires who might have called him out on strikes.

Never once did I ever hear Jim Northrup give a pitcher credit for having made a good pitch. Hell, a guy can fall on his ass in baseball seven times out of ten and still be a hero. But to hear Northrup tell it, making an out was never his fault. The blame always had to go somewhere else.

Much as I despise Ted Williams, he did give credit to the pitchers. But Northrup, no way. Northrup would be mad coming to the ball park on Monday just because it was Monday and we had a game to play. I've always felt Jim hated himself, and on the rare occasion when he did crack a smile, he hated himself just for smiling and temporarily ruining his image.

Playing on the same teams with Jim Northrup for a lot of years, both in the minor leagues and in the majors, I think I got to know him pretty well. Or as well as I could stand to know him. And I think that down deep inside himself, Northrup always thought of himself as being a superstar. But he never had superstar credentials. Not even star credentials. Not once. Not ever.

Someone said Ted Williams got a good look at Northrup early in Jim's career and made the observation that there was

0

no reason in the world why Northrup couldn't be a .300 hitter.

The hell there wasn't. The reason was Northrup himself. He had the most acute case of red-ass I ever encountered not only in a baseball player, but in any human being I've ever met. Mad at the world, seven days a week, that's our boy Jim.

He roomed with Mickey Stanley for a long time and he was always taking cheap shots at Stanley. Now, Mickey's always had this good-guy, all-American, clean-cut image which I never bought anyway, but Northrup was forever riding him about it. Northrup always was one of the chief agitators on the club, but he had the shortest fuse of all. The man simply couldn't take it like he could dish it out.

Jim was a streak hitter. He'd get into horrible slumps, then into tremendous hot streaks. I benefited a lot from Jim's hitting when he was hot, and he won a whole lot of games for me with his bat. Once he was on the field, I'm sure he never gave a thought to his personal feelings about anyone, and he was a fiery competitor who'd bust his gut to beat you—but Northrup was playing his own game for his own satisfaction.

It was odd that Northrup and Stanley would be roommates.

Hell, they couldn't stand each other. And Stanley's front—the nice-guy, Jack Armstrong bit—was a bit hard to swallow. I always felt he was the biggest backstabber on the club, and I never wanted to say anything around him that I didn't want repeated. My trouble was, I always thought those little wise things after saying the very unwise things, and always fretted too late about who heard me when I popped off.

Stanley's always been basically a good defensive player, but at the plate I always thought he had a fear of the baseball. He just bails out on everything thrown at him. If I could have spent a career pitching to Mickey Stanley, I'd be around longer than Satchel Paige. Just pitch him outside, and every once in a while brush him back just to make him think, and you own him.

Like I said, whether I dislike Northrup or Mickey Lolich more intensely is a toss-up. Lolich's trouble is that he was blessed with a million-dollar arm and a ten-cent brain. He's another guy who kept himself from greatness. He's a good competitor, but down deep he's a spoiled brat. The Tigers always babied Mickey, and Mickey just grew to love it.

I got to know him a little bit during spring training of 1963 and he spent most of that season with the big club while I spent all but the last three weeks in the bushes. My first full season with the Tigers I won four games, Mickey won eighteen.

0

From then on, until the roof caved in on Dennis Dale, Mickey could never win as many as I did. And I'm convinced the rivalry that he manufactured between us kept him from being as effective as he might have been.

The fact that I was a bigger winner, a bigger star, and thus got more attention, really riled him. He became a crybaby and, much like Northrup, always had an excuse for a losing performance. Without fail, it was someone else's fault. Mickey generally blamed it on his teammates for their failure to hit behind him. When I had my biggest years, Lolich went around dropping snide remarks to the press about the lusty hitting the Tigers turned in when I was pitching. He could win thirty-one games, too, if he had that kind of hitting. Shit, he couldn't win thirty-one if he spent the whole season pitching against the House of David. And with precious few exceptions, he'd lose the clutch games his team absolutely had to win.

Lolich was blessed with one of the finest arms I've ever seen. Most pitchers would take weeks in spring training just getting to the place where they felt comfortable throwing their curve ball, while Lolich could snap them off the first day in camp. The good Lord simply gave Mickey an outstanding arm. Too bad He didn't give him more of an ability to think on the mound.

Had Mickey Lolich concentrated more on opposing batters, and less on his personal battle with Denny McLain, he'd have been a bigger and more consistent winner over the years.

He had the one great fling during the 1968 World Series, but other than that his career has been marked only by its inconsistency.

While we're talking about southpaws, there's another left-hander who'd be on my list if I ever made up a roster of people I'd like to punch in the mouth. Hank Aguirre was with the Tigers when I came up from the minors and he couldn't hide his resentment. Hank's one of the most petty guys I've ever encountered. He had no curve ball, a minimum fast ball, a horseshit slider, and a decent screwball when he could find the plate with it.

I'm convinced that Hank's inability to think cost the Tigers the 1967 pennant.

When I first came up to the club, Aguirre was there along with Jim Bunning and Phil Regan. Regan turned out to be a great guy, and very helpful. Bunning was cool to me, but after all he was the big gun on the staff. Besides, I liked him because he was outspoken. He was testy all the time, but he knew how to pitch and he knew how to win. Aguirre was in the majors on a shoestring anyway, and I figured out his hostility right away. He figured every young player in the Tiger organization was out to get his job.

Aguirre was the leader in the clubhouse humor department. Had he given the same concentration to pitching that he did to making his teammates laugh, he'd have been hell to beat.

Aguirre and Charlie Dressen hated each other. Charlie was a masterful judge of talent and he knew a loser when he saw one. One night in Kansas City, Dressen and Aguirre engaged in the most heated shouting match I've ever witnessed in baseball.

Dressen's "gopher" was Wayne Blackburn. Blackie was listed as a coach, but all he did was run errands for the manager. Blackie was a little guy with a crooked smile and all he wanted in the whole world was to please Charlie Dressen. And it was, "Blackie go," "Blackie sit," "Blackie run," "Blackie get this," "Blackie do a bedcheck."

One night Charlie told Blackie to check the rooms to see if anyone was out past curfew. A few were. The late group included Aguirre, Cash, and Kaline. Now, they seldom checked Kaline's room because he always had that good-guy image, like Stanley. Dressen always checked Aguirre because of his hatred for him. More than once Charlie had warned Hank, "Don't you ever let me catch you out past curfew or it'll be your ass."

Well, Charlie did catch him, and it definitely was Hank's ass. We had gotten our rear ends trimmed that day, and Dressen was plenty pissed. I was rooming with Joe Sparma at the time and, for some reason known only to God, we happened to be in our rooms well before the deadline.

When Blackie checked Aguirre's room, there was no Hank, and Blackie, like a good little doggie, reported the good news to Charlie Dressen. Charlie headed immediately for Aguirre's room. You could hear him coming all the way down the hall, and just as he turned the corner, the elevator door opened and out stepped Kaline, Cash, and Aguirre. Kaline ducked into our room to wait out the storm we all knew was coming.

The two of them—manager and pitcher—went at each other in a verbal tirade that must have roused the entire hotel. It was incredible the way they were yelling at each other. Hank was urging Dressen to trade him and Dressen was saying,

0

"Hell, I've tried to get rid of you ever since I got here, but no one will have you." The whole thing lasted at least ten minutes, and Dressen's last words to Hank were, "You asshole, you won't be here twenty-four hours from now."

Charlie couldn't make good that promise. Apparently it was true—no one wanted Hank Aguirre. And he was still with the club when Charlie Dressen went to his grave. And Charlie went there still hating Hank Aguirre.

Next to my own success, the success I rooted for most in all my seasons in the major leagues was Joe Sparma's. But for the most part, success eluded Joe. He and I roomed together for a while and he remains one of my great friends.

The Tigers expected magnificent things from Joe in the season of 1968 and they had every reason to, since Joe had a 16–9 record the previous year. But he never could put it all together and wound up dividing twenty decisions when we won the pennant. We used to call him Greasy Joe because of his Italian heritage, but the nickname that finally stuck with him was Ralph Williams. Believe me, Joe was just like that West Coast car dealer—he had a deal a day, and most of them were bad.

Funny thing, Joe really believed in every one of them. He always thought he was going to strike it rich.

Joe was blessed with a superarm and he was such a lovable guy, it was impossible to dislike him, even when he got us involved in some of those screwy deals. In fact, it was Joe Sparma, with a little help from Al Kaline, who got me involved with attorney Ed May.

Joe could never understand why he didn't become a big winner, but Joe's really not an athlete in the ordinary sense of the word. I know he played quarterback for Woody Hayes at Ohio State and all that, but all one of Woody's quarterbacks has to do is get the snap from the center and hand the ball to another back.

Sparma wasn't a free-flowing, fluid kind of athlete. He just couldn't move his body. His maneuverability was limited. It was really funny to watch him pitch. He threw some of the greatest fifty-two-foot curves in baseball history. They'd be fine in the Pony League, but in the majors it's sixty feet six inches from the mound to home plate.

One time in Yankee Stadium he had men on base and Freehan called for a pitchout. Hell, Sparma threw it into the backstop. Yankees were running around the bases laughing their asses off.

In all the years he pitched, Joe never was able to get any consistency and, as a result, always suffered from wildness. And when he was off beam, he couldn't find home plate with radar.

But Joe was always good for a deal.

I recall one road trip that took us from Anaheim to Minnesota before coming back to Detroit, and Sparma insisted that we meet with these two guys to discuss a hot deal. I was feeling rotten, battling a case of the trots, hitting the john about every ten minutes. But nothing would do. We had to see these guys, because they were gonna make us rich. And Sparma never lost his optimism about these deals. If one failed, he'd be twice as enthusiastic about the next one.

So we not only had to meet these guys, we had to impress them as well. We ordered a bottle of scotch and a bottle of vodka sent up to our room. Joe was convinced it was better to talk business in the room rather than in a crowded restaurant.

Dressen was managing then and he dropped by our room about seven that evening to check on my health.

"How you feeling?"

"Brutal."

"Better hit the sack early. Drink some liquids and see if you can flush that stuff out of you."

With that, Charlie was gone.

Then our guests arrived. By midnight, the scotch was gone, the vodka bottle was half empty, there were cigarette butts and dirty glasses all over the place, and we went to bed, me convinced I was definitely going to pass away before sunrise and Sparma convinced that financial independence was lurking around the corner.

I didn't die, Joe didn't get rich, and the only thing lurking around any corner was Manager Charlie Dressen. He was truly a thoughtful guy, and he came back to our room bright and early next morning to check again on my health. This time, he didn't ask a single question. Instead, he took one look around the room at the mess and walked out, muttering, "Don't bother explaining anything, you guys, because there's no fucking way I'm about to believe either one of you bastards."

Sparma and McLain never had any luck at getting by with any of our little tricks. We never, ever quit trying, though. Joe may get upset at reading this, but he and I are a lot alike. We both absolutely love life, every minute of it, and firmly believe in living every minute of it to the fullest possible extent.

Our families have been close, too. Our kids are about the same age and we had great fun with them. And even though we missed our wives and kids when we traveled, each of us looked forward to going on the road trips because we made each other laugh, even when parts of our worlds were crumbling.

One of the players who introduced me to some pretty good card games was Jake Wood. He never made it big in the majors and I'm not at all certain it really bothered him. Jake the Snake did two things—pinch running and playing cards. That was his whole life. We played mostly night games, so every afternoon in the hotel you could count on a card game, and you could count on Jake, Gates, Willie, and McLain being involved.

Daryl Patterson is a guy who helped us in relief in the 1968 season and here's a guy who made it to the big time without the hint of a curve ball. When he didn't have the good heat, he was in a pile of trouble.

Pat Dobson gave everyone a nickname and the one he picked for Patterson was "The Chief." I think Daryl was part Indian, but even if not, he surely promoted the old legend that Indians can't handle whiskey. Daryl would get high just walking toward a bar, and when he got a couple in him he thought he was Sitting Bull. Wanted to whip everyone in the house. Fortunately, he was a very funny guy to be around and there were always other players nearby to keep Daryl pretty much in line when he started acting like the heavyweight champion of the Cherokee Nation.

A modern medical miracle is Norm Cash. Here's a guy who abused his body for so many years he should turn it over to Mayo Clinic when he's through with it. Amazing specimen, Cash. Norm would go early and stay late, yet somehow show up every day not only eager to play, but madder than hell if he didn't get to. He hustled his butt off to stay in the major leagues, and if not for a lot of guts and determination might have been destined to spend his entire career in the bushes. I always felt better about everything when I looked over and saw Stormin' Norman at first base, even though I'll confess I sometimes wondered how he managed to remain in an upright position.

But he wanted to win, and to play, so badly, that I'm certain

0

the psychological took over where the physical left off. I always felt Norm Cash got turned on by the fans.

Another guy with an immense desire to play, and one to whom God gave only minimal skills, is Dick McAuliffe. What a great guy! He was just as fiery as he appeared to be. I always admired Dick for his competitive attitude. He didn't want the other team standing after a game. He not only wanted to win, he wanted to win decisively. Here's a guy who made himself a major league player simply through hard work. Too, he plays golf cross-handed, and still hits the ball 260 yards, right down the middle. And he's just as competitive in card games as he is on the field. He simply doesn't like to lose at anything.

The finest defensive shortstop I've ever seen is Ray Oyler. At the plate, he was helpless. I mean, he couldn't hit his way out of a room full of toilet paper with a crowbar. But the thing I'll always remember about Oyler is that he knew he was a horseshit hitter, he'd tell you he was horseshit at bat, and he never pretended to be anything but horseshit. But the way he could field, I'd keep him on my club if he couldn't hit his weight. And Oyler couldn't.

Ray and I were roomies when I was riding highest. He did everything for me, and we got along tremendously well. I loved him dearly. He had practically no success at all in baseball and knew all along his fielding kept him there, but never once did he resent the good things that were happening to me. Come to think of it, maybe Ray was a lot better off. The press didn't bother him, he had no fast money deals coming his way, and all he had to worry about was getting to the park on time.

The fact that he made it, all the time, is a tribute to modern science. Oyler had a history of a bad stomach and he practically lived on liquids, and I don't mean milk. He ate just one meal a day, and that was with me. We either ate a late breakfast, or grabbed a bit before going to the park late in the afternoon.

The man simply loved his beer. I don't know, maybe it helped him forget about his batting.

Ray tried everything to become a good hitter. Nothing ever worked. The man never once in his life even had so much as a decent hitting streak. The average player gets twice as many hits as strikeouts. Not Ray. In 1968 he got only twenty-nine hits all year, but struck out fifty-nine times.

Oyler tried stances no one had thought of before. He was

open, closed, widespread, narrow, you name it. Whenever he spread out, he couldn't get out of the way of the baseball so he changed that one around in a hurry. I'm certain Ray had a great fear of the baseball, except when it was hit at him.

All through the '68 season, Ray volunteered to be my telephone answering service on the road. He used to kid me about it:

"Now, roomie, we both know the only call I'm ever gonna get is if I'm sent back to the minors. On the other hand, you need your own secretary on the road, and I'm elected."

Sometimes he'd signal me while I was on the phone and demand to talk with me.

"Don't tell 'em everything, roomie. Remember, tomorrow's another day and you have to save something to tell 'em at tomorrow's news conference."

One time early in the '68 season Mayo Smith announced a workout for 10:30 A.M. the following day.

"Is there anybody here who can't make it?" he asked.

"For Christ's sake, Mayo," bellowed Oyler, "I'm not through throwing up every day until eleven o'clock!"

Ray's glove work (we led the league in fielding that year) was greatly responsible for our winning, and my heart ached for him when Mayo announced he was going to use Mickey Stanley at shortstop in the World Series.

That's the only time I ever saw Ray Oyler pissed, and he had every right to be.

"I play all fucking year out there and we win the pennant and now when we get into something that's really meaningful, something every kid dreams about all his life—but God, I'm not good enough to be a part of it."

He said that privately to me, in our room. Publicly, to my knowledge, he never uttered a word, but it cut him deeply. Mayo had used six different people at shortstop during the season, but Ray had played twice as much as any of them.

He never got an official at-bat in the World Series against the Cardinals, although he was in four games for defensive purposes. The only time he came to the plate, damned if Mayo didn't order him to lay down a bunt. And Ray did it, perfectly, and without bitching.

Hindsight is a wonderful thing, but I'm sure the Detroit Tigers would have done just as well in the Series with Oyler at shortstop. Stanley made two errors, batted .214, and didn't drive in a single run.

O

Dick Tracewski (who later became a minor league manager in the Detroit system, then still later a coach for the Tigers) played shortstop some of the time in 1968. All the guys knew he was nothing but a pipeline to the front office. Anything he heard went right to the manager or to the front office. Maybe getting to be a coach was his reward for that faithful service.

Later on, he rented my house in Lakeland when he was managing down there and ruined my indoor-outdoor carpeting. Still owes me two hundred fifty bucks for it, too.

Pat Dobson was a guy whose record didn't indicate his worth to the 1968 Tigers. He won only five games, but he started and relieved and did a good job on the field. His main value, though, was in the clubhouse. Dobson had a good mind, and he kept everybody loose. He invented nicknames for everybody—for instance, for Jim Price, our second-string catcher.

One day Price popped into the clubhouse and announced he wanted to be called The Big Guy.

"Never happen," screamed Dobson. "Any way you want to look at it, you don't qualify for that nickname. Not physically. Not mentally. Not behind the plate. Not at bat. Nowhere, Price. Your nickname is Thunderthighs and you're stuck with it."

Indeed he was.

We'll just run down a list of some other guys I've played with at Washington, Oakland, and Atlanta, and I'll give you capsule comments on them.

Hank Aaron: Great hitter, quiet, very much a loner. But I think some power groups have gotten to him in the last couple of years because the things coming out of Hank Aaron's mouth don't sound like the Hank Aaron I knew.

Mike Lum: We called him "Mr. Hawaii." A legitimately nice guy. There were lots of nice guys on the Atlanta club. That's probably why we didn't win.

Ralph Garr: One of the most gifted athletes I've ever seen. He can hit, run, field, not a great arm but a good one, and he never missed the cutoff man. Besides all that, he loves to play. The only thing bad that ever happened to Ralph Garr was Dusty Baker.

Dusty Baker: When he started influencing Garr, they became the Katzenjammer Kids. If Dusty didn't always look for trouble, it always looked for him. And found him. There's no question about it, the Atlanta ball club had a racial problem when I was there. There was tension on the club all the time, and there were more weapons in that clubhouse than they had at Fort Dodge. Dusty got Garr started on that black power bull-shit, and let's face it, white guys don't like that because they're accustomed to having all the power.

Earl Williams: The biggest joke in baseball. If he ran forty feet on a routine ground ball, it was a lot of running for him. On a popup, he never even threatened to run. A player owes it to himself and to the fans to make it appear he's making an effort, anyway. Williams never tried to disguise his laziness. If Earl Williams ever gets to be as good as Earl Williams thinks Earl Williams is, then Earl Williams will not be in major league baseball, he'll be in heaven directing traffic. And if he makes that, he'll be lazy at it, too.

Bernie Allen: The Wizard. Could have been a truly great player if he hadn't had that bad leg all the time. A super guy who says exactly what's on his mind. That's why Ted Williams couldn't stand him.

Mike Epstein: It's a pity someone smart didn't work with Mike because I'm convinced he could have been one of the best hitters in the game. He was no all-star with the glove; matter of fact, he didn't particularly care about going for pop flies. But a good sound hitter and a nice man.

Sal Bando: A quality player who goes about his business and does it all pretty well without making a lot of noise.

Reggie Jackson: Good player, but he won't be great until he starts to use something besides raw strength at the plate. He could be a truly great hitter if he'd work at it. Reggie's one of the game's all-time hot dogs and the players don't like him, but he can hit the shit out of the baseball.

Darold Knowles: Every club has a Louella Parsons and Darold will fill that role wherever he goes. Great rumormonger; then he'll go around denying he said anything in the first place.

Blue Moon Odom: As long as Charlie Finley owns a major league team, you have to figure Blue Moon will have a job. He's always been the pipeline from the clubhouse to Finley, and everyone knows it. First thing I was told when I joined the Athletics was to keep my mouth shut around Odom unless I wanted the front office to know about it. Charlie Finley never needed to come to the locker room to learn what was happening as long as he had Odom and Frank, the clubhouse man.

Ken Holtzman: One of the truly great spirits of all time. The most lovably crude man in history. Every other word he utters is "fuck." I think he's in love with the word. He'll go out of his

0

way to put in into a sentence. Sometimes he'll put it between syllables of a word. It's just a thing with him.

Bert Campaneris: Very moody, but very talented. Very difficult to understand, but everyone can understand those base hits he gets and the plays he makes at shortstop.

Dick Green: Nice guy. He'd rather be moving furniture somewhere in South Dakota. His wife hates baseball and she's been after him for years to give it up.

Joe Rudi: Everyone says he's underrated, but who the hell underrates him? He's a good player who goes about his own business in a methodical way, does his job, and wants to be left alone. And everyone pretty much leaves him alone.

Catfish Hunter: I used to wonder how in the hell he ever won a game. His fast ball is ordinary and his breaking stuff isn't all that good. But he knows what he's doing out there, and he has excellent control. Good guy, too.

Vida Blue: I should thank him for getting in some time with the Oakland club. If he hadn't been having that trouble with Finley, it's not likely the A's would have called on me. Great arm and a super fast ball, but he'll never be a really outstanding pitcher until he comes up with some good breaking stuff.

Looking back on all the major league clubs I played for, I'd have to say I was in Oakland long enough to wish I could start all over again, in Atlanta long enough to see the end of the line, in Washington long enough to learn how to hate all over again, and in Detroit long enough to realize my dreams.

THE GARBAGE

5

IN MY LIFE

I've been an adulterer and a gambler. I suppose I've broken just about every one of the Ten Commandments.

Now, I haven't committed murder, but maybe I've worried some people nearly to death.

The difference between Dennis Dale McLain and most other people is that my sins have been right out in the open, partly because I've been in the limelight and partly because I really haven't made much of an effort to hide what I am or what I think.

I'm a male chauvinist pig, no doubt about that. And I always will be. I think a woman has three places she's well suited for: the bedroom, the kitchen, and wherever it's necessary to be to take care of the home and the kids. It's that simple. I don't think she should even be allowed on a golf course and, with rare exceptions, not in government or in any position to make important decisions. I simply don't think women are emotionally equipped to make big decisions.

As we write this book, I'm married. I probably will be married to Sharyn Boudreau McLain for a hundred years. But our relationship, if it were to be described by a counselor, would be called turbulent. It's been a combination of heaven and hell. Quite honestly, Sharyn has given the heaven and I've provided the hell.

Right now, we're legally separated, and God only knows how long that'll last. She's been living in Chicago and I'm back trying to make a living in Detroit. But I go "home" every weekend, because "home" is where she is, and where my four children are. As far as women go, I married the best. And my home means more to me than anything in the world.

But my marriage has been rocky off and on ever since we got married. More than likely, it'll continue to be that way. Whatever problems we have, I'm to blame, one hundred and ten percent.

My problem is that I am not capable of giving of myself. I've always believed it goes back to my childhood. My dad died when I was just thirteen years old, and seven months later my mother remarried. I resented the guy she married and I resented her for marrying again. I felt betrayed, and I felt my father had been betrayed.

Let's make this clear right now: My folks were happy together and they were true to each other. She had every right to get remarried and to try and build some kind of a life for her family. But at the age of thirteen, I was incapable of understanding that. All I knew was that I missed my dad, and I didn't want anyone else, any outsider, interfering in our lives.

Maybe my bitterness that grew over the years makes me a lousy husband. I'm sure my childhood experiences contribute to it.

The plain truth is that I have tried to make it up to Sharyn by giving her material things and an excitingly different life. She'd agree it's been different, anyway.

But the thing Sharyn has wanted most in life is me—and that's something I just cannot give. Once you become a public figure, you simply have no life of your own. And I'll be frank about it, I like being a public figure. I like being recognized—except when I'm someplace I shouldn't be. I like the spotlight and the things that the spotlight can do for you. Well, most of the time, anyway.

The only way I can really show my love for Sharyn (and I'll love her always) is to buy her things. When I was growing up, my dad didn't make very much money and, while we weren't on welfare, there were a lot of things we simply couldn't afford. After he died, it was more of the same.

I made up my mind that if things ever got rolling for me, I'd have everything I ever wanted. I feel the same way about doing for my wife and children. The practice has been this: See something they need or want, and they have it. Nothing very complicated about that.

As for my business deals when things were going good, she didn't know about 99 percent of them. And that's the way it should be. A woman has more than enough to worry about, just taking care of the house and the kids. She shouldn't have business on her mind.

It's not that I think tending to kids and a home are simple tasks, rather they are noble ones. Sharyn has gone through more real encounters with life than any wife of any automobile executive in Detroit or any corporation wife in New York. And everything considered, she's come through it beautifully, even with all the hell I've put her through. She finds it difficult to live with me, but I know in my heart she'll always love me. And there's not another woman in the world who could ever take her place.

I confess I've done some pretty extensive research in trying to find a replacement for her, though. There you have the root of our problem. I've been an unfaithful husband. Sharyn is, and always has been, a jealous and possessive wife.

O

I remember doing a television show in Detroit and another guest on the show was Dollie Cole, whose husband Ed recently retired as president of General Motors. Mrs. Cole was making a big fuss over how difficult it is for an executive's wife, what with all the travel and stuff.

Hell, she doesn't know what hardship is!

She's a spoiled millionaire and she almost made me vomit with those stupid statements. She's had things done for her right and left; and when big-time executives have to move their house is sold for them and another one bought for them. Baseball wives have to move two or three or more times in a single year. The club gives you so much money for moving expenses, and that's it, brother. It's up to you to uproot your kids, get them into another house and another school, and hope to God you get off a road trip in time to help them get settled.

And you must understand this: If you're an athlete, you travel. If you travel, you're going to face temptations. If you're successful as an athlete, you're going to have more temptations, even if you're as ugly as a mud fence.

When things were rolling, you'd have to admit, I was a pretty successful athlete. And when you're going good in one league, you go good in all of them. The temptations are tremendous, and every once in a while, they'd overcome me. They'd chew me up and spit me out, and time after time Sharyn found out about them. Sometimes it was because I was careless and stupid, sometimes because I made the mistake of going to bed with a loudmouth broad.

There are two things that can wreck you at the house and at the office, whether your office happens to be an executive suite at General Motors or a pitcher's mound. Those two things are sex and gambling. Their contributions to my downfall, I'd say, were about equal.

Let me say this about gambling: It's a necessary evil, generally it's a victimless crime, and it should be legalized, here and now, all over the United States. I don't see anything wrong with gambling.

And if it is wrong, you're still not going to stop it. So we should legalize it, and get the schools and hospitals and roads and libraries and services we need in this country.

I've been gambling since I was five or six years old, and I dig it. I love to play cards, I love to bet money on bowling, on pinball machines, and I'm drawn to the tables in Las Vegas and Reno and Tahoe like a hog to slop.

0

People have been gambling since the beginning of time. The soldiers gambled over Jesus Christ's garment, and people will be gambling over something the day the world finally comes to an end.

I first started playing penny-ante poker around the house before I went to school. We played pinochle, and later when I started into baseball I learned some new games like gin rummy and hearts (I confess the learning process was an expensive one).

Some of the purists argue that money from gambling goes into organized crime to support the drug market and stuff like that, and I'm sure some of that is true. But why not legalize the whole shooting match, and run the bookies out of business entirely? It's a proven fact that since New York came up with off-track betting, it's hurt the bookies' business.

Why the hell is it legal to go to a racetrack and put money through a pari-mutuel window, but illegal to bet on the same horse in the same race with a bookmaker? I don't understand the logic to all that.

Some states have started to get wise by establishing a lottery, and that's an intelligent first step in the right direction.

Now, I know some people get hooked on gambling like others get hooked on booze or drugs. Hell, there's help for those people. Let the gambling addicts go to Gamblers Anonymous. If you cut your arm, you go to a doctor. If you're an alcoholic, you go to Alcoholics Anonymous. But the average guy doesn't get hooked, and for him, gambling is not morally wrong.

I grew up thinking it wasn't wrong, and I still don't think so. I actually didn't do much gambling when I was in high school. I styled myself as a pretty good bowler and I'd bet a dollar or two with other kids my age, and I'd win. Then I got into a pot game with some older fellows, and learned pretty quickly I wasn't ready for that league.

When you have only three or four dollars in your pocket, and you lose half your money in one game, you learn pretty quickly when a game is too rough for you. God, how I wish I had retained that early lesson when I got involved with the really big money later on in life!

I think every person is pretty much responsible for his own morals, or lack of them, but the people you hang around with in your early days have a profound effect. I took money for playing baseball back when I was in high school. A fellow on

O

the South Side of Chicago agreed to pay me ten dollars a game for playing on his team.

In theory, it was supposed to be for gasoline money, since I had to drive a considerable distance to get to the games—then all of a sudden the guy screwed me around and refused to pay me the money, so I quit. Funny, even at the age of fifteen (I had my driver's license early) I met up with a bad thief. At about the same time, the Firemen's Club in my home town of Markham was paying me five bucks a night to play softball.

I worked all through high school, and the only real gambling I did was in the check pool every Friday. All the workers put a dollar into the pot, and the best poker hand out of the check numbers won the pot. I worked at the O-Cedar Mop factory for eight months and never won that damned check pot. I should have gotten some sort of message out of that.

The first substantial bet I ever made was a fifty-dollar plunk-down on a harness horse at Maywood Park in Chicago. This was after I had signed a baseball contract and had come home after playing winter baseball.

My Uncle Bob, who was on the Chicago police force, got a hot tip from one of his friends.

The horse ran in the shithouse. You see, I kept getting one message after another about gambling, but it never soaked in, not until I had been kicked out of baseball.

I really got introduced to card games the following summer, my first season of organized baseball in Clinton, Iowa. We had a first baseman by the name of Bill Decosta. He must have been thirty or thirty-one years old then, and had never made it to the major leagues. He loved to play cards, and some of the other guys on that team, Cisco Carlos, Buddy Bradford, Bruce Howard, Joe Cherry, and Bob McKillop, they all were involved in the game. So that was the beginning, but I didn't lose much money because they were small games and I didn't have much to lose anyway.

The poker games really got serious the following winter in the Florida winter league. The White Sox minor leaguers stayed at the Sarasota Terrace Hotel and the big game was called Between the Sheets. It's not a dirty game, like it sounds. It's a high-low game and there were always eight or ten guys in the game.

I remember Ken Berry, Jerry McNertney, Mel Howard, and myself were always in the chase. The White Sox really frowned

84

0

on gambling and if Farm Director Glenn Miller had found out what really was going on in those hotel rooms he'd have kicked all of us in the butt. Al Weis, the superstar of that team, was in the games, too, and so was a kid named Andy Rubilotta. Andy was a smart hustling guy from New York. He had just signed for a lot of money and he roared into Sarasota in his slick new 1962 Thunderbird.

We used to kid McNertney a lot. He must have been twenty-one or twenty-two years old then, and he was still a virgin. Later on, he came up with the White Sox when I was with the Tigers, and at age twenty-six I think he was still a virgin, except that later on he got to where he was really proud of it.

McNertney never hit much, but he had a great arm.

That Between the Sheets game was very popular in the major leagues. I've heard stories that some big league teams have some really heavy games with guys betting their entire paychecks on the pot.

I really didn't bet much money in the early days. Hell, I didn't have any money. When I came back from winter ball in 1962 I had exactly seventy bucks in my pocket, and went to work for the Fuller Brush Company to make ends meet. Can't you picture me walking up and down Kenworth Avenue and 55th Street, knocking on doors? I was a beauty. Hardly sold a brush.

In 1963 I was with the Tiger farm system. My salary went up a little bit, and so did my gambling. We had some pretty good shooters at Duluth. There was Jim Rooker; Pat Jarvis, who later went up with the Braves; and Tom Timmerman, who later pitched for Detroit.

But at this stage of my life, I hadn't really made a big bet of any kind, on anything, and had never met a bookmaker.

Charlie Dressen is the man who really introduced me to the finer points about handicapping. Charlie was a great man and I loved him almost like a father. And Charlie loved the ponies.

There are tons of stories about Charlie, how it wasn't uncommon for him to make five or six thousand dollars a day at the race track.

Charlie taught me how to read the *Racing Form.* I had some good times with him at the various tracks around the country. Maybe we got along well because each of us is a gambler at heart. Charlie spent lots of time at the track, and I remember he had a tip on a horse at Thistledowns in Cleveland

0

one time and couldn't get to the track in time because he had a luncheon commitment, so he just sent one of the players out with his bet.

When I first came up to the Tigers I heard stories that Paul Richards, when he was managing a bad ball club in Baltimore, frequently would deliberately get himself thrown out of games just so he could get to the track in time to make a few bets.

Charlie Dressen was not nearly as liberal about sex as he was about gambling. It's been said of Charlie, and it is absolutely true, that he was "anti-blow-job."

"They'll either kill you or they'll drive you crazy," he used to say. "Either way, you're just as useless. Get laid all you want, but stay away from those blow jobs."

Most guys never listened to Charlie's advice on sex.

Baseball players are funny about their sex, though.

Personally, I learned, the hard way, that it's not good for me to have sex the night before I pitched. And even the players who cheat on their wives rarely did it on the final night of the road trip. The theory was they'd then have a little more left for the wife.

I had my first sexual experience when I was in high school. Some guys introduced me to the leading ladies at a house of ill repute. I had fooled around a little before that but I really had no idea what I was doing.

At the whorehouse, I didn't have to. My hostess knew enough for the two of us. She also knew something that I didn't know: She had crabs.

That cured me for a while and I never fooled around again until my first year of baseball in Clinton, Iowa. I didn't know a hell of a lot more then than I did back in high school, but I was learning.

The greatest sexual experience I've ever had has been with my wife. We've been married more than eleven years now, and I still get excited every time I think about her.

The first time I cheated on Sharyn was quite some time after we got married. The Tigers were on the road, in Minneapolis as I recall. It must have been in 1967 or 1968, because I was going good, and when you're doing well, you have the pick of the litter.

Being a male chauvinist pig, I like to be the hunter. Being hunted turns me off. But once in a while I'd let a girl take advantage of me. The first time it happened I really felt shitty. I

0

remember I was coming home the next night and I wanted to blurt it right out and tell Sharyn.

But she had been jealous and possessive right from the start, and I figured she wouldn't handle it too well. Because her father had played baseball and she had been exposed to that kind of a life, I thought Sharyn would be more understanding than she has been about all the temptations a traveling athlete has to face.

So I didn't tell her, mainly because I didn't want to hurt her. But I think she knew it anyway. She met the plane, and on the ride home I was unusually quiet. Normally I'd be talking her leg off, but this time the ride home was different. She asked me several times what was bothering me. No way was I telling her.

It was a long time, though, before I cheated again.

Besides, in the next few seasons I was too busy winning baseball games and making appearances and putting together deals to worry about broads. I was accused of screwing around a lot, but it just didn't happen. If I had been to bed with 10 percent of the women I'm credited (or blamed) with having, I'd be down to ninety pounds. And I'm nowhere close to that.

One of the scariest times I ever had in my life was during the 1969 season. I was pitching well, and flying my plane all over the place, and getting the paint company going, and doing all sorts of things.

In a weak moment one night, working late at the office, I took a quick trip to the couch with one of the secretaries. It was wham, bam, thank you, m'am, and nothing more. Besides, she was married. It's the first and only time I ever touched her. Next day she rushes into the office and announces she's in love with me and wants to leave her husband.

I tried to explain to her the difference between lust and love.

"It'll grow into something beautiful," she said, "if we give it time."

Unfortunately for her, that's the one commodity I had too little of and, as far as I was concerned, that ended our little relationship.

It was a one-time shot, but it was just about the costliest number I've ever done.

The previous winter, when my musical group was flying home from an appearance, we were chatting with the stewardesses as we always did. One of the girls was particularly nice.

O

Just nice, nothing more than that. Everything on the up and up.

She was based in California, and as we got off the plane I told her, "Hey, if you ever have a layover in Detroit, give us a call and come see us." Nice. Simple. Gentlemanly. Nothing dirty about that. Right?

A couple of days after the little trip to the couch, the stewardess called and I invited her to grab a taxi and come over. She did; I came out into the reception area and gave her a big hug. I figured it was the only decent thing to do.

Well, let me tell you, my secretary grabbed me by the shirt and turned me around and accused me of "two-timing" her! Can you imagine that? She ranted and snorted around the office for a while and finally I took her aside and explained the facts of life:

"Look, you're married and I'm married. It's gonna stay just that way. This is a girl all of us met on a plane. She's just an acquaintance, nothing more. Now, you're a super secretary, but this thing has gotten out of hand, and I don't think you'd better come back to work."

Nice. Firm. Cut and dried.

No. None of those things. I was not nice, she was firm, and she wanted me both cut and hung out to dry. She did her best to get me that way. She went straight from the office to my home, sat Sharyn down and told my wife that she and I had been engaged in a long and dramatic romance.

Well, there was none of that, "Hi, honey, how did your day at the office go?" stuff when I wandered in.

Sharyn's a tiny lady, but she seemed to tower over me. I had no chance to even begin what I thought would be an explanation. I had rehearsed several possible stories during the drive home.

Sharyn was crying and screaming, and I couldn't reason with her. My associate at the time, Eddie Demetrak, was with me and I kept hoping he'd come up with something, a funny story, anything. It seemed like hours before either of us could get a word out. Finally she stopped to catch her breath, and I began trying to explain the whole thing and how people were ganging up to destroy me.

I gave her the old "Hell hath no fury. . ." routine, but she was having none of it. She was leaving and taking the kids and that was all there was to it. She was convinced beyond all doubt that I had been unfaithful and no amount of pleading could dissuade her.

O

"I should get your gun and blow that thing of yours right off," she threatened.

I tried to be cute. "Fine, if you have to shoot me, shoot me there. I could live somehow without that thing, but if you shoot me in the head or in the heart, it's all over."

She's a bright girl with a good sense of humor, but this day her funny bone was missing.

She finally quieted down, I think from sheer exhaustion, and we crawled into bed.

We had made a resolution years ago—like many couples do—never, ever to go to sleep mad, never, ever to close our eyes with a cloud hanging over our marriage.

Needless to say, the promise went out the window that night. Sharyn went to sleep resolved to take the children and leave me. I was capable of enduring anything but that, and I rolled and tossed a long time after she fell off to sleep.

Sometime in the middle of the night I awakened in a cold sweat. Everyone has had that experience, I'm sure, knowing that someone is watching you while you sleep. I knew Sharyn was awake. I also knew there was a gun in the house. I had been dreaming that she was about to blow my brains out.

I was afraid to open my eyes. I felt something on my head and for all the world it felt like the business end of a .38 revolver.

Here's a two-time Cy Young Award winner about to close out his beautiful career in bed, in a pool of blood. Beautiful.

I made a bold decision—that it was better, and certainly more manly, to die with my eyes open, facing the music. I opened my eyes and Sharyn was awake and sitting up all right, but it was her hand, not a gun, on my brow. Apparently my restlessness had awakened her and she mistook what was a fearful and cold sweat for an attack of flu.

There were other bad dreams, real ones. Like the girl I met when I was pitching in Birmingham in 1972. When I got called up to Atlanta, damned if she didn't leave her husband and move to Atlanta, too. Sharyn and I had not been getting along, but I had not seen Rhonda in a month. I simply hadn't called her. I was trying to put the pieces of our marriage back together.

One day I was home with Sharyn and the kids, and there was a knock at the front door. I looked through the little peephole and there stood Rhonda. Another bad dream. Another cold sweat. But I had to open the door, and in my most businesslike voice I inquired, "May I help you?"

0

"You're damned right you can, you sonofabitch!"

"I'm sorry, lady, he doesn't live here any longer."

And I slammed the door in her face.

For some queer reason, Sharyn didn't quite buy that act.

The incident that put me in the deepest water in Atlanta was one in which I was totally innocent, though. I was opening a night club in Atlanta, and our license went into effect on New Year's night. I had worked around the clock to get the place ready and we had invited everybody in town.

And it seemed all of them showed up. There were broads of every size and shape, and let's face it, you have to have broads if you're going to have a successful joint.

I had been drinking all day and could barely stand.

That evening, about nine o'clock, Sharyn called and announced she'd be down soon for the opening. Fine. Nothing wrong with that.

Nothing, except that when she walked through the door, I was giving a bear hug to a—well, to what you might call a bear. I told you we had invited lots of ladies. The one I was hugging looked like someone who was disqualified from the roller derby for being too fat and too tough.

She was just a nice girl who wanted a hug, and it was a friendly hug and nothing more. In fact, hugging her was a full-time thing and required a considerable amount of patience.

Patience. I had it. The fat, ugly broad had it. Sharyn didn't. She came in just as we were locked in this tremendous embrace and there was no explaining the thing.

Had I known my little wife was going to perform in such a manner, I'd have put on a cover charge. She used language that I thought only I knew.

Soon afterward, Sharyn packed up the kids and left me.

I did some tall talking to get her to come back.

You know, there are three things that get athletes in trouble: booze, broads, and betting. I had two of the three going pretty steadily and how I ever kept from having a drinking problem I'll never understand.

Sharyn has known about other women, mostly because of my own stupidity. And my own lust, naturally.

Players generally get caught either because the "other woman" calls the wife, or because they bring phone numbers home on a piece of paper. I'm guilty of that, too.

There was a young woman named Mary whom I had met on a plane. After all, planes can be lonely places and everybody

0

should have someone to talk with. So we talked, then we had a toddy, then we started fooling around. Then Sharyn found Mary's telephone number in my shirt, and you know the rest: Sharyn called her and they had what you might describe as a very animated conversation.

Later on, I was in Washington during the off season and was just leaving my hotel room for an appointment. Some people were waiting for me in a car downstairs and I was late. As I was going down the hall toward the elevator, the phone in my room rang. I raced back to the room and answered it, all out of breath. I was in such a hurry that when Sharyn and I hung up, I neglected to say, "I love you." Now, I've always told Sharyn, "I love you," when we wind up our phone conversations. This time, I didn't. There was no reason on God's earth except that I was in such a rush.

Next time we talked you could hear the ice water rushing through Sharyn's veins.

She didn't buy my explanation that I was out of breath from running back to the room. She thought she had made a call at a bad time and that she was interrupting something.

Hell, I'm not at all sure I'd interrupt *that* for a phone call.

Athletes' wives are pretty prolific, if not original, at making telephone calls to other women. Possibly the greatest game athletes and their wives play is a sort of "hide-and-seek" game involving telephone numbers.

Let's face it, if you get a hot number in some town, you want to save the number because with any luck at all you're going to be returning to that town a lot of times.

Hiding a phone number someplace where it cannot be found is not easy. For the wives, finding it apparently is. I've often wondered if the wives all get together in little skull sessions and exchange notes on how best to go about digging up those phone numbers and recognizing the telltale signs.

Of course, most athletes are so stupid their wives don't have to be too tricky to figure out their extra-marital moves.

Sharyn called another girl. Her name was Linda and I had met her in Texas after the Washington Senators were moved there. Since I figured I was going to be playing there, I was trying to line up a television and radio show in Texas. Some friends introduced me to her. Some friends!

The problem with Linda was that when I was traded to the Oakland Athletics, she thought she was a part of the trade. She picked up her duds and moved to Oakland. Sharyn didn't have

0

to conduct much of a search to find out about Linda. As I recall, I left her telephone number lying around in the wide open spaces and, sure enough, Sharyn called her.

Wives have pretty much a set pattern to these calls.

Generally, they get the broad on the phone and say, "Hi there, I'm a friend of Denny McLain and I'm trying to get in touch with him. Can you please tell me where I can find him?"

Beautiful!

Funny thing, though, I could never, ever care for any woman other than Sharyn. We've been married since October 5, 1963, and even today I get turned on just thinking about my wife.

I know, then why do I cheat? All I can say is that I am normally weak. The flesh is weak. But, nobody's perfect.

I really think my sex drive helped me make it to the major leagues.

Right after I signed with the Chicago White Sox, I was sent to Harlan, Kentucky, to play for a team in a rookie league. Much as I wanted to play organized baseball, I hated to leave my girl in Chicago. We had gone together quite some time even though we had not really had sex together.

By the time I was in Harlan I still hadn't been to bed with her, but I was obsessed with the thought of doing it.

In my first game of organized baseball I pitched a no-hitter and struck out sixteen batters. Would you believe that the very next day, I was officially in trouble with the front office? Sure, you'd believe that.

I was feeling pretty cocky over my first-night heroics, and a trip back to Chicago to see my girl friend seemed in order. I borrowed a car from a catcher named McDonald and drove the 600-odd miles to Chicago. I visited my friends and my girl, then someone pointed out an article in the Chicago newspaper. It seems the White Sox were wondering where I was.

One call to the front office prompted me to hightail it right back to Kentucky. Glenn Miller assured me that if I pitched well the next time out, the White Sox might be able to arrange for me to play somewhere closer to home.

A few nights later I struck out sixteen more and even though I didn't give up an earned run, I was beaten 2–1. But it was enough for the White Sox to promote me to Clinton, Iowa. Two hits and thirty-two strikeouts in eighteen innings was proof enough, and I was on my way.

It's really not that far from Clinton to Chicago, so I brought

0

my car to Clinton and the first thing I did after pitching a game was to hop into my car and run home to see my girl. My manager at the time was Ira Hutchinson, and no sooner had I returned than he informed me I would be fined a hundred dollars if I made that trip again.

No one tells Denny McLain what to do, right?

The next night I was back in Illinois, and the following morning Ira informed me I owed the club a hundred bucks. I couldn't figure how he knew. I decided to try it some more. And he caught me again. Another hundred.

I waited until one thirty in the morning before leaving on my next little excursion. No one would dare follow me at that hour.

As it turned out, no one had to. As I crossed the bridge and paid my toll, I noticed the bridge attendant taking down my license number. The bastard was calling the manager!

I was making five hundred bucks a month, and the fines for the first month totaled four hundred. Those were tremendously expensive trips, especially when you consider I was returning to Iowa with nothing to show except a bulge in my slacks.

The only solution was to get married, so my girl came to Clinton. We tried to elope to the same town in Michigan where Sharyn and I later were married, but the justice of the peace informed us we'd have to wait three days. So we drove all night to get back to Iowa only to find her parents waiting there for us. They accused me of kidnaping her, and promptly shuffled her into their car and drove her back to Chicago.

I saw her only a couple of times after that because soon after this experience I was discovering I was really in love with Sharyn.

A little more than a year later, we got married.

Our honeymoon lasted only two days before I had to go to Dunedin, Florida, to pitch in the Florida winter instructional league. By this time, I was the property of the Detroit Tigers.

Sharyn had to return to her job at a bank in Chicago and she was to join me ten days later in Florida to resume our honeymoon. It was a week or so before I had to pitch. The schedule called for me to pitch on Wednesday night and my bride was to arrive two days later. She called Monday night and told me she could come down early. I met her plane on Tuesday night and we quickly began rediscovering each other. The discovery process took all night.

When I went out to pitch the following night, I couldn't

0

stand. My knees were hitting each other and I was starved. Whatever stamina I had, I left it in our bedroom. That night I learned a lesson, and that is never to have sex the night before pitching. Later in my career, when the fast ball was gone anyway, I abandoned that rule, but by then hardly anything mattered and I was trying to enjoy whatever I could.

Back then, I was making $350 a month and Sharyn and I were broke all the time. I couldn't have bought a low-necked dress for a hummingbird.

Somewhere along the line Sharyn and I had heard that if you put a penny in a jar for each time you make love during your first year of marriage, then take two pennies out of the jar each time you make love after that first year, the jar will never be empty.

After thirty days in Dunedin, we didn't have enough money to put food on the table. So we sat down and talked about our financial situation as two immature kids will do. We decided we had no choice except to bust open the penny jar.

We counted 118 pennies!

Not bad, considering that we had been married just thirty days.

Until the next paycheck arrived three days later, we lived on bread, mayonnaise, and Pepsi Cola. The good old days? They were pure hell then, but they look a helluva lot better as you grow older.

If I could have stuck to pennies in the jar, and penny-ante poker, there's no telling where I'd be today.

Sharyn never knew much about my gambling. She knew I liked it and was doing it, but she never asked any questions. And I never volunteered a thing, particularly when things went sour with that operation in Flint.

When I was with the Detroit Tigers, gambling was as much a part of road trips as the baseball games. Card games are a ritual, not just with the Tigers, but with every baseball team. The guys who played most when I first came with the club were Hank Aguirre, Jake Wood, Gates Brown, Dick McAuliffe, Jerry Lumpe, and Willie Horton.

I was no Oswald Jacoby with the pasteboards.

Matter of fact, I was such a fish in the early stages of my major league career my teammates nicknamed me Dolph, short for dolphin.

Even though the games were pretty stiff sometimes and

0

guys could lose two or three hundred dollars at a crack, they were friendly games. No one complained, except Jim Northrup, and Jim complained from the time he got up in the morning until he went to bed that night.

A typical game was seven card high-low with five dollars the maximum bet and three raises tops. I learned to love the game, and loved the action of gambling even when I lost consistently.

I even worked up a bowling bet against my father-in-law. Lou Boudreau had a bowling team in Chicago so I got up a bunch of guys from my neighborhood and we decided on a home-and-home series, each side putting up five hundred bucks.

The first series was in Chicago and they whacked us good.

Now, getting beat at anything is tremendously distasteful to me, so for the return match on my lanes I rang in a couple of ringers, one of them being a pro, Dale Seavoy. Needless to say, we got even.

In the winter of 1967–68, I was bowling seven nights a week. I don't know whether all that exercising of my right arm and shoulder during the off season helped strengthen me for the thirty-one-victory performance in 1968, but it certainly didn't hurt.

It was pretty common knowledge that Dennis Dale could be talked into making a bet on his bowling, so one evening I was approached by a guy who allowed as how he might be persuaded to bet. I had seen him throwing the ball around, and he didn't look too tough to me. So we started rolling and betting. He was knocking pins into the next county and I was putting the ball right into the pocket and wasn't getting shit.

Before I knew it, this clown emptied my pockets.

I demanded a rematch. I guess it takes a while for something to sink in with me. Next time, I insisted we bowl at *my* favorite lanes. We broke about even that time.

I found out later—about $600 later—that in our first engagement, they were using extra heavy pins and he was using an eighteen-pound ball. I was using my personal bowling ball, a standard sixteen-pound ball. He'd throw his ball and mow those pins down like duckpins, but those pins were so heavy my ball would hit them and it seemed my ball was almost coming back to me.

The Dolphin strikes again, or gets struck.

0

I thought I had gotten even with him, though, because the check I gave him bounced. But this guy was no slouch. He called the general manager of the Tigers and made certain he got his money.

Bowie Kuhn won't like this, but I did a bit of gambling while sitting out my suspension. I had nothing but time, and so I spent most of it on the golf course and got pretty good at the game.

Most I ever won in a single game was a thousand dollars. We had pretty much the same group of golfers all the time, and all good friends—Burl Wilson, Don O'Malley, and Patrick O'Shea, all pretty good shooters whichever way you want to look at it. I also played a lot of golf and bet some pretty good money against the told-time pitcher, Rip Sewell. He was a pain in the ass because all he did for eighteen holes was piss and moan about how unlucky he had been, and how lucky the modern baseball player is. He insisted the players of his era were so much better than today's athlete; so I enjoyed beating the crap out of him and taking his money.

On one occasion, I threw a golf match.

I had been playing for quite a bit of money around Lakeland and there was a guy who spent considerable time at the golf course. I can't recall anything but his first name, Fritz. First time we played, he told me he could play me even. The way he shot that day, George Shearing and Stevie Wonder could have walloped him, and I took him for about seventy dollars.

Next time out, we settled on my giving him two shots, and I still beat him out of fifty bucks or so. He gave me thirty and told me he'd have the rest on Friday.

By Friday, I learned he had been making $25,000 a year but had been fired, and was on workmen's compensation. Now, here's a guy trying to get along on eighty bucks a week and he's losing twice that much to me playing golf.

He came back that afternoon, cashed his unemployment check and handed me the twenty. Damned if he didn't want to play again. He told me the whole story, that he had been making good money, that he had lost his job and that he had a wife and four kids to support.

There was no avoiding another game with him, so I insisted he take four shots a side. He beat the daylights out of me and I lost $40. When I paid him, I told him we'd never bet again. Mentally, I just couldn't get myself together to play him. He was

0

busted, but at the same time I was suspended, with no money coming in except whatever I could hustle, and I could ill afford to throw my money away in a sympathy bet against him.

Whoever said Denny McLain was hardhearted?

THE WITCH
DOCTORS
6

A long time ago I heard a joke about a hunter who had been shot by one of his hunting companions. The pellets from the blast of the shotgun at close range riddled the fellow not only where it hurts most, but where it counts most. From the moment of the blast it was obvious the victim would never sire another child.

His companions loaded him into a station wagon and tore down the road.

"Are you taking me to a doctor?" he asked.

"No," said the friends, "we're taking you to a piccolo player in the next county. He can teach you to finger it so you won't pee all over yourself for the rest of your life."

The more injections I had in my arm and shoulder, the less humor I found in that story. Even today I'm amazed I can shower without the water leaking through from one side to the other.

I had arm trouble just once as a youngster. I had just finished my freshman year at Mount Carmel High School and some of the players from our baseball team joined another league in the Chicago area. I started messing around with a dinky little curve ball and my arm began to ache. I didn't pick up a baseball for three weeks. I never had what you'd call arm trouble until I was in the major leagues, and once I got it there, I can't say that I ever really got rid of the trouble.

Another time, when I was eleven or twelve, I banged up my shoulder when I wrecked my bike. Later, when I was examined for high school football, doctors discovered the shoulder had been broken.

I decided that if I ever made anything of myself in athletics, it'd have to be something other than football. From then on, all my energies went into baseball.

The day I originally hurt my arm in major league baseball was July 26, 1965. By coincidence it was the first time I had pitched against Bruce Howard, the pitcher the White Sox decided to keep when they made me available to the Tigers. It was the second game of a Sunday doubleheader. The first game dragged on for more than three hours, and the White Sox beat Mickey Lolich 10–6.

It was a terribly hot day and we ripped Howard out of there in the second inning with seven times. By that time we were leading 8–1. I think it was about the fifth inning when we scored a couple more, and between innings the temperature dropped about ten or fifteen degrees. It didn't get freezing,

0

don't get me wrong. But it turned from very hot to semicool. We had taken a long time at bat, anyway, and when I went back out to the mound I didn't take very long in warming up.

First batter of the inning for the White Sox was Pete Ward, and on the very first pitch I threw to him I felt something pop in my shoulder. I finished the game and did pretty well, but I had a sore shoulder to show for it.

Norm Cash hit a couple of home runs that day, and Dick McAuliffe and Jerry Lumpe also hit them to make my job a lot easier. I recall saying to the writers after the game that four home runs each game was the secret to my success. I promised that if I got that much hitting help every game, I'd win twenty with no sweat.

The following morning, I felt like I would never win another game. I could barely raise my arm, so when I went to the park I checked in with our trainer, Jack Homel. He had rubbed some muscle soreness out of me in times past, but this was no ordinary problem. He knew it was more serious than the normal stiffness that most pitchers get after they've pitched.

Homel suggested I go see Dr. Clarence Livingood, one of our team doctors, at Henry Ford Hospital. And Dr. Livingood set me up with Dr. David Mitchell, Sr. He told me a shot of cortisone might do me a world of good. Fine, doc. Whatever you think is fair. I'd never had cortisone before, but I'd had penicillin and it couldn't be worse than that, right? Wrong!

With all the preparations they went through, you'd have thought I was headed for major surgery. A nurse scrubbed my shoulder and put a towel over it to keep it sterile. Doc Mitchell explained the process. First, I get a shot of xylocaine to freeze my shoulder, then I get another shot of cortisone. "You might feel me moving around with the second needle, but it's an anti-inflammatory drug and we want to make sure we spread it around."

He suggested that I turn my head the other way and not watch the process.

He needn't have given me that advice. I hate pain, especially my own, and I've always been scared to death of needles. The thought of getting two of them back-to-back had me grabbing the nurse's hand and holding on for dear life. Sure enough, the xylocaine worked, and when he put the second needle in, I could feel him moving it around, but I really didn't have any pain.

The doc walked away, so I figured he was all through and

turned around. Don't you know that frigging syringe was sticking up in the air, right in the middle of my shoulder? Jesus, Mary, and Joseph! I nearly lost my cookies and passed out right then and there. It turns out he hadn't injected the cortisone yet, so he came back and started probing around. I could actually hear the needle hitting something down deep inside my shoulder.

Walking out of Ford Hospital that day was more of an escape than an ordinary release. But two days later I felt super. Whatever he gave me got rid of the inflammation, and I became a great advocate of cortisone. From then on, every time I had anything from a sore arm to a chest cold, I wanted cortisone.

Later—two years later—when my arm really started giving me fits, cortisone shots were pushed on me, but it didn't take a lot of pushing for me to run down and get a shot in the shoulder or arm. I'd tell Mayo Smith or the trainer I was having some soreness, and the word was, "Well, you'd better run down and get a shot."

It became a ritual. Pitch. Get sore. Get your shot. Pitch some more. Get another shot.

I had shots from one end of the American League to the other, from my neck to my hind end. I had just the one shot in 1965, four or five the following season, ten or twelve in 1967, and tons of them the year we won the World Series.

One of the truly great guys I met in all my years in baseball was Dr. Russell Wright. He was one of the team doctors for the Tigers, too, but the only cortisone he ever gave me was in 1967 when I hurt my foot.

Doc Wright has retired now, but I'd bet he's still one of the strongest men in the world. His treatments were sometimes worse than the ailments. He had the strongest hands in the business and since he was an osteopathic physician, he was a great believer in physical manipulation. Many times he rubbed a lot of soreness and tons of aches and pains out of my body, sometimes even during a game when I'd give him a signal and meet him in the clubhouse between innings. He treated me beautifully, but I always kidded Doc Wright that when he got someone on the table, he thought he was Clyde Beatty taming a wild lion.

Don't get the impression all these cortisone shots were forced on me. They were promoted, not forced. And I encouraged all of it. I knew I had to win baseball games to make money and to support my wife and kids. I would have done any-

0

thing in the world to keep pitching. But right then and there, as far back as 1967, I realized my years in the major leagues were limited.

It was always Doc Wright's theory that my trouble was caused by a radical overdevelopment of my right, or pitching side. And I think perhaps he's right. With all the pitching I had done since I was a kid, and the tremendous amount of bowling and other activities, my right side was much more developed than my left. Doc said this overdevelopment caused problems that could only be cured by manual manipulation. And then the cure was only temporary.

A doctor in Washington, Dr. George Resta, had another theory. He thought my brain was out of whack. Here's a guy who's been the team doctor for the Senators and Redskins over a long period of time, and who was a big medical wheel with the United States government when Dwight Eisenhower was President. He thought my problems were imaginary. So instead of giving me the cortisone that I wanted, he'd give me a shot of Vitamin B-12 and tell me it was cortisone.

I always wanted to consult with Dr. Robert Kerlan of Los Angeles. I knew he had prolonged the careers of Sandy Koufax and Elgin Baylor and probably lots of other athletes, but so much was happening I just didn't get around to it. The Tigers didn't recommend that I see him, and if they weren't going to pay for it, damned if I was going to do it on my own. I was in enough financial trouble at the time without running up a bill with Doc Kerlan.

Later, when I was with the Oakland Athletics, owner Charlie Finley suggested I go to Mayo Clinic and do whatever was necessary to get the thing fixed. All I could think of was that some doctor was going to recommend surgery, and I couldn't bear the thought of someone cutting my arm or shoulder. As it turns out, I should have had surgery. It's obvious to me now (as are so many things, too late) that I had so strained the tendons and ligaments over a period of years that nothing short of surgery was going to help. Doc Kerlan even told my coauthor a few months ago that some kind of surgery likely would have been possible and that it surely would have helped ease the discomfort that I feel even today, even if it never got me back to my best pitching form.

What's the old saying, we get too soon old and too late smart?

Doc Livingood once advised me to take a whole year off

and rest. That was the only solution, he said. That was obviously out of the question. I could hardly afford to stop going for a day, not to think of a year.

Doc Wright gave me X-ray treatments. I've had diathermy and deep therapy, rubdowns and rubins—you name it. Fans used to send me all sorts of remedies through the mail. One time I got some wild-smelling ointment from someone on the West Coast and put some of that stuff on my arm. Man, it smelled like cowshit on a hot summer's night, and I had to go out there and pitch a baseball game smelling like that! I couldn't stand myself! So I poured cologne, after shave lotion, and deodorant all over my shoulder trying to get rid of that odor, but it hung on for the whole game. As I recall, I won the game. The batters probably were anxious to get up there, get their cuts, and get the hell back to the dugout.

I had so many X-ray treatments in Detroit in 1968 and 1969 I thought about getting an apartment close to Detroit Osteopathic Hospital. The treatments didn't hurt and they lasted only a few minutes. They kept charts on how many treatments I had because I guess if you have too many of them you can get sterile. The way things happened later, being sterile, or at least impotent, might not have been a bad alternative.

Nothing I tried gave me anything more than a little bit of temporary relief. I simply got reconciled to pitching with pain. I don't think there's ever been a pitcher in baseball who hasn't had some pain in his arm. You simply can't throw that many baseballs over a long period of time without doing some damage to your arm.

Except for Hoyt Wilhelm and Satchel Paige. I always figured they had plastic arms, anyway.

I appreciate everything that all the medical, and some of the nonmedical, people tried to do for me. I'm certain they had my best interests at heart. But every doctor had a different theory. Problem was, none of the theories worked on me.

Athletes are a fairly superstitious lot, and many of them had theories, too. It's happened to me lots of times: A teammate knows a guy who knows a guy who knows this doctor. He's a little eccentric, but he gets results. Try him. You'll like him.

My lovable teammate with the Oakland A's, Ken Holtzman, had the simplest theory of all: "Look, all this stuff is bullshit. If

0

your arm is a piece of shit, it's a piece of shit, pure and simple. Fuck it. You know what I mean?''

Certainly. There was never any doubt at all what beautiful Ken Holtzman meant.

But his arm wasn't sore. Mine was. And I was willing to try anything.

Reggie Jackson said he knew a guy in Chicago and another guy in Arizona, where we were in spring training. Nearly every guy on the team really tried to help, because Vida Blue wasn't in camp and the club needed another pitcher. Finally I bought Curt Blefary's story.

It seems a doctor Curt knew had a radically different theory about these cortisone injections. He didn't insert the needle where the pain was (and my pain for years was always in the same spot); Curt's man was convinced you had to get down to the *origin* of the pain. With that elaborately simple theory, he quickly became *my* man. Beautiful. Just fucking beautiful. Finally I've discovered a man who's gonna get to the bottom of this trouble and, whoosh, make it disappear with one simple treatment.

It was about as simple as mathematics was for me back at Mount Carmel High.

The doctor explained his theory to me: The nerve endings in my shoulder were inflamed, and these nerve endings all had their roots in one central nervous point, and that point, he figured, was on my upper back, just underneath my right shoulder blade.

Sounded logical to me. I wanted to quit hurting so much that the more illogical the proposition, the more sense it made. Seems I carried that thinking over into my business transactions at one time or another, too.

The cure-all meeting was set for a Sunday afternoon. The doctor had a condominium near our training site. After Curt introduced us, we sat around and chatted for a little while until he said, "Are you ready?''

He asked me to sit backward on a straight-backed chair, then he put his finger on a nerve I never knew I had, right underneath the shoulder blade. The minute he pushed hard on whatever it was he found there, I shot out of that chair like the Great Zucchini.

I'm telling you, I never had so much pain in my life, and he still hadn't put the needle into me! I was off that little chair like

O

popcorn, racing around the room with the doctor chasing me. We broke a lamp and an end table, and I don't know what else we turned over. Every time he touched that spot, I yelped and ran.

After fifteen minutes, the doctor—whom I was beginning to dislike just a trifle—was certain he had located the right spot for the miraculous injection. Hell, I could have found a cure for cancer in that time!

Blefary finally had to sit on my lap, on the chair, while Dr. Wizard worked his wonders. When time came for the injection, I jumped up screaming and knocked Blefary right on his ass and began racing around the room with that damned needle sticking out of my back.

Wouldn't that make a great scene for a movie? But if they do it, they'll have to get Duke Wayne to play my part. I'm not going through it again, even with fake needles.

The good doctor did all this without any pain-killing drug preceding the cortisone shot. Ruins the effect of the healing drug, he said. Damned near ruined my head and his ceiling.

If I had pitched at all well that spring, I wouldn't have consented to all this. But I had been getting the crap kicked out of me. I mean I couldn't get Molly Putz out.

Curt had been nagging me about seeing this miracle worker, and my last time out, seeing all those line drives whiz past my ear, convinced me.

Funny thing, I pitched the day following that treatment and threw the hell out of the ball. I didn't win; I think Cleveland beat me 2–1 or something like that, but I went seven strong innings. Like everything else, it didn't last. Maybe I pitched well that next day because my back was so sore it took my mind off my shoulder.

Twice in two days, I thought I was dying. First, when the doctor did his thing on my body, and the next day flying down to Tucson. The Oakland manager at the time was Dick Williams (one of the world's great front-runners), and he gave me permission to fly my own plane down to Tucson where we were to play the Indians. A former schoolteacher of mine was hosting a television show in Tucson and had asked me to stay over and appear with him. So Williams okayed my plane trip.

It was only eighty miles or so. I filled both my gas tanks before the trip. I was alone, flying at about seven or eight thousand feet, digging every minute of that kind of freedom, singing

0

to myself and telling myself what a great voice I have. Then I happen to glance at my fuel gauge and it's reading one-quarter full.

Somewhere, there has to be a fuel leak. Either that or a little gas-guzzling gremlin has stowed away with me. One look out my window told me what was wrong. The rubber liner on the gas cap on the right wing was worn off, and I could see the fuel running out of the tank.

"You crazy bastard," I thought aloud. "What a way to go. Here you are, singing a happy tune, and you're running out of fuel. You'll either run all the way out and put this thing down in a grove of trees, or the whole mess will blow up in your face and there won't be enough left to identify the remains."

I quickly switched to 121.5, the emergency circuit, and yelled for help.

"This is two-six-eight-four Sugar at seven thousand feet, requesting emergency landing instructions. I have a fuel leak and I have no idea how long I can hold out."

You have trouble in your car and you can pull off the road and get out and take a look. Up there, you just don't pull over to the side of a cloud and check things out. As it turned out, I had enough fuel to make it to Tucson, but not enough time to get it fixed before I had to go to the ball park. I did the pitching, the television show, then headed back to the airport and finally located a mechanic who assured me he could do the job for me.

He did, and I headed back up into the wild blue yonder for the trip back to Phoenix. Approaching Phoenix is a beautifully eerie sight because of all the surrounding mountains. I was in the middle of them when I happened to check my fuel gauges again. They read a quarter-full again. And I had filled both tanks in Tucson!

Back I go to emergency again, and I had to make a pretty good climb just to make sure I could coast over the mountains in case I ran out completely. Luck was with me again, and I made it safely back to the airport, only to discover that the mechanic hadn't tightened the gas cap.

Two near-misses on one trip! My arm may have been a piece of spaghetti, but my rear end was in one piece.

When time came to sit down and prepare the material for this book, I made up my mind to speak frankly about every-

0

thing. At the same time, I decided that every man is the custodian of his morals, so I'm not about to divulge darkly hidden clubhouse secrets nor tell who does what to whom nor make any moral judgments.

This is no "clubhouse confidential," and there'll be no naming of names. I've said before that in many respects, the athletes of the world are a great deal like your ordinary person: They feel the same anguish and despair and thrill to the same things that a "civilian" does. I doubt that they're any worse, or better, morally than any other group of people. Naturally, the temptations are greater than in many fields of endeavor, and it is true that for the most part, baseball players are not college educated since most of them signed contracts right out of high school.

But, basically, I have found, people are the same everywhere.

There's been a great deal written and said in recent years about the prevalence of drugs in athletics. Some of the stories are alarming, but many, I think, have been exaggerated. There are twenty-five players on an average baseball team, and I'm convinced that almost any group of twenty-five housewives consumes as many "uppers" and "downers" as a baseball team in an average season.

I never heard of any player using drugs when I was in the minor leagues. The only time I had anything you could call a drug-related experience in the minors was in 1963 when our Knoxville team was playing a game in Nashville. I had a miserable cold and a fever of about 103 degrees and a headache that wouldn't quit.

I had to pitch that night (well, I don't suppose I had to, but I felt I had to, anyway) so I started taking Excedrin. I took two of them about four in the afternoon and didn't feel any better. So I took two more an hour later, a couple more about six thirty and a couple more right before the game. Count them, that makes eight Excedrin.

I was on cloud nine. We won the game 4–1, Northrup hit a grand slam home run and I struck out sixteen. So perhaps you could say I was drugged, but I didn't take those pills to get high, I took them to try to shake the effects of the flu.

It was either 1965 or 1966 when I first became aware that some of my teammates on the Tigers were given to occasionally popping a "greenie." A greenie doesn't have to be green, but I guess the term has been used because the original amphetamines that were kicking around major league club-houses were that color.

I guess they come in all colors and strengths now. You can't say that every guy in baseball has popped one at one time or another, but it's safe to say that every guy has at least a nodding acquaintance with them. Now, every guy in the world is going to deny ever having taken one, or even having seen one. That's ridiculous, but then again you can't expect a bunch of major league players to line up and volunteer for drug reha-bilitation just because they popped a greenie now and again.

I suppose there are some guys who never took one in their lives. Others popped a few. Some others had so many of them around they resembled traveling pharmaceutical companies. I've played with some guys who took them as regularly as brushing their teeth. Some more frequently, as a matter of fact.

As for myself, I've probably popped a dozen or fifteen over the course of my career. I haven't made any detailed study of the stuff, and I'm certain that over the long haul they're not good for you, but there's no question but what they're popular, and they do something for you psychologically if not physically.

Just as a housewife pops a diet pill not just to lose weight but to gain energy, so it is not uncommon for today's modern athlete to consume a greenie now and again.

The toughest stuff I ever took, though, was a solution called "red juice." I learned about it when I joined the Atlanta Braves in what we'll call the twilight of my career. It's dynamite! It's the most bitter tasting stuff I've ever had in my system, but it is an unbelievable potion. You get the idea you can go through walls, and all you need is a sip.

The taste? Imagine a cross between vinegar and bourbon whisky. It's that bad. Made me want to choke first time I tried it. I nearly vomited all over the clubhouse.

One of the Atlanta veterans introduced me to it. He gave me a sip out of a pint bottle of the stuff. If anyone who was on that Atlanta team tells you he wasn't aware of it, then he's not aware this is the twentieth century.

It was a liquid amphetamine and I finally got a doctor to give me a prescription for some of it. A shot of that stuff and it makes you believe that you can throw a baseball through a house. The first time I took it was just before a night game, and it was eleven the next morning before I could close my eyes and go night-night. Sexually, you become something of a cross between Errol Flynn and Robert Redford. Because it's in liquid form, it gets into your bloodstream right away, and in eight or ten minutes you're fully prepared to whip the world. You find yourself talking a mile a minute.

My first bout with it went for naught because we were rained out. The next time, I consumed an ounce of the stuff before a game I was to pitch against the Cincinnati Reds. I got beat 3–1, I believe, but it was the best game I had pitched in a long while.

My third, and last experience with red juice came on a Sunday afternoon. I had been out late and was dog-tired and I figured between me and the red juice, we could stay awake for nine innings. I could have avoided the whole process.

It had to be 100 degrees in Atlanta Stadium at game time and my body temperature seemed like it was twice that. I got belted out in the first inning—and still had eight or nine hours to go before that crap wore off! It was disastrous. That's it, one, two, three times with the red juice and no more, and I wouldn't advise it for anyone unless you happen to be in a dull town and want to get to the moon in four minutes.

I don't think marijuana is now or ever has been a big thing among major league baseball players. I never knew about the stuff, except what I had read and heard, until I joined the Washington Senators in 1970. Someone from the office of Commissioner Bowie Kuhn had lectured all the teams about the evils of drugs, and had warned that anyone caught messing around with the stuff would be considered guilty of high crimes against baseball.

The Washington club had gotten off to a great start that year, then fell into its customary tailspin. As we began a road trip in Milwaukee, we had lost something like ten out of twelve and lovable Theodore Williams ordered a strict curfew. Every man in his room by midnight. And everyone was.

As I went to my room about ten thirty at night, I heard some guys laughing in the room across the hall. I knew they were our guys, so I knocked on the door and they let me in. The smell that came out of that room would have knocked over a bull elephant. There were two of our fringe players in there, and they were laughing their asses off and didn't care who heard them. They had big shit-eating grins on their faces and were puffing away on those funny cigarettes. They asked me to join them but I declined.

Over the years I've heard rumors about two or three players

0

who allegedly were on hard drugs, like heroin, but of my own knowledge I'm telling you I don't know of a single case. In reality, I don't think the amphetamines are a big problem, either. A few years ago, before the government came out with all this publicity and banned the manufacture of certain "uppers," I think some players did some babbling about them. Big talk, you know. But like most big talk, it was highly overrated.

It became the "in" thing. I've heard guys say, "Man, that greenie really moved me up a length," or, "I'll need to pop a greenie so I can stay awake once we get to the West Coast."

In all the years I spent in the major leagues, I knew only three players who drank to excess. In each case, they were either fringe players, or older players hanging on to the shred of a career that was fast fading.

I've never been much of a drinker. The first drink of booze I ever had in my life came when I was nineteen and pitching for Duluth-Superior. I had just won a big game, and someone was throwing a party at the VFW hall and we were invited.

Hell, I didn't know what to order. Mike Cloutier and Jim Rooker were along, too, so they suggested I try several things until I found something I liked. I tried beer, scotch, bourbon and gin, and didn't like any of them. But while checking them out, I got severely plowed under. I mean, I couldn't find my ass with both hands.

We were five to a room in that league, as I recall, and when we got back to the room there were four other guys trying to get out of my way. I was convinced I'd have to die in order to feel better.

All I really remember is the room starting to spin around and around, and Rooker telling me to lie on my stomach and put one foot on the floor to stop the spinning. Damned if it didn't work.

I've been drunk just one other time, and that was the night we won the pennant. I had been taking antibiotics for a heavy chest cold. At about the seventh inning, we knew we were gonna clinch it that day so I kept sneaking into the clubhouse dipping into the champagne we had waiting for the celebration. By the time the game was over and the troops came roaring into the locker room, I was in a stupor. It was funny watching television films of our locker room celebration, and seeing myself trying for what seemed to be hours to get the cork out of a bottle of champagne. I was so drunk I couldn't make a fist. I

0

later wound up at the Lindell A. C. bar in downtown Detroit, then somehow found my way to a tavern out in the suburb of Dearborn. How I finally got home remains a mystery to me.

Even today, I'm not much of a drinker. I have an occasional taste of vodka and grapefruit juice, but if they quit making the stuff tomorrow I'd be the last guy to suffer.

Drugs? I've tried them, and I don't like them.

CHARLIE AND TED
AND THOSE IN BETWEEN

7

I broke into professional baseball in 1962.

By 1972 the good years and the good times were gone and I was through. And by that time I had been taught by, played for, fought with, babied by, and driven nearly insane by fifteen managers.

Perhaps an athlete like Bill Bradley or Jerry Lucas or Mike Marshall could make a study and determine the relative strengths and weaknesses of managers and their value to or damage to a particular team.

I got along with most managers. In some cases my relationship with them was more of a cold-war standoff. With others, there developed a great admiration and friendship.

Charlie Dressen knew more baseball and could communicate more of that know-how to his players than any man under whom I played. Now I've heard great things about other managers like Walter Alston and Paul Richards and I always regretted that I didn't play for Earl Weaver and that the White Sox didn't keep me around so I could learn more from Al Lopez. But in this chapter, I'm going to comment only about the managers who managed, mismanaged, or decided they could not manage me.

It's been repeated so often that folks tend to believe the theory is true, and that is that managers affect the outcome of only seven or eight baseball games a season. Hell, who ever came up with that figure? Some managers can win twenty or thirty games for you through lots of methods, mainly through the proper handling of pitchers. Others who can't tell the difference between sheep manure and cherry seeds couldn't manage a fart after a bean dinner.

Every manager I ever played under was human, except for Theodore Samuel Williams, and these managers utilized different methods in trying to get the job done. But the business of getting the job done largely is in the hands of the players on the field, and there've been some damned good baseball teams that won despite the presence of a bad manager.

And I'm equally convinced that some good teams were inspired, driven, or what have you to great performances because of the skilled handling they got from a manager who made a study of the game, his opponents, and his own personnel.

Face this fact first: It's extremely difficult for a manager to be a tremendously popular guy simply because he can only play nine guys at a time. That means there are sixteen

0

grumblers sitting on the bench thinking they should be in the starting lineup. So it's not an easy job; it's one with lots of built-in avenues to unpopularity.

How many managers are given testimonial dinners?

Who's the main target for the abuse of the fans?

Mayo Smith was the manager of the Detroit Tigers when we won the pennant and the World Series in 1968, but the poor guy never got the proper credit for the job he did. I think Mayo was the ideal manager for that kind of team, and did a masterful job of handling the guys.

On the other hand, possibly the most praised man in modern baseball history, maybe of all time, is Ted Williams. For my money, he's the most incompetent and uncouth man I've ever encountered.

As a kid, and a baseball fanatic, I idolized Phil Cavaretta and Bob Rush and Mickey Mantle and Ted Williams. I played briefly under Cavaretta and pitched against Mantle and got to know him pretty well. Those guys proved to me that baseball players are human. Williams proved they're inhuman, too.

You want to know the first words Ted Williams ever uttered to me when we met face to-face for the first time?

"What's dumber than one fucking pitcher?"

Hell, what was I supposed to answer? I didn't have to. Teddy Ballgame had all the answers.

"I'll tell you what. It's two of you dumb fucking pitchers."

Isn't that a dandy way to start a relationship?

I've said that I try not to hate anyone, but if I ever make up a list, Ted Williams will be right up there. Whatever I have done wrong in life, I atoned for it in the one season I spent playing for Ted Williams in Washington. I prayed for an injury, or anything that would get me away from that gibbering idiot. If I had known anyone in the Mafia, as I have been accused of knowing, I swear I'd have had one of those goons stomp on *his* feet—or mine so I wouldn't have to pitch for him.

Managers use different methods to get the best possible performances out of their players. Williams had one method that he applied to everybody—it's called fear.

I'm not bright enough to figure out whatever deep-seated hangups the man may have had left over from his childhood or from his tangled personal life, but he thrived on intimidation. And I mean he intimidated everyone—his players, coaches, the press, and the fans.

During the season I played for the Washington Senators

0

there were but two nice things that happened in my relationship with Williams. One was being on the disabled list for twenty-one days, and the other was a workout he missed because he went on a hunting trip.

You could tell from the very beginning our relationship would be a testy one. I'm no shrinking violet, either, and when I went to the Washington club the "Dennis the Menace" thing had been reasonably well established. The trade took place during the World Series in early October of 1970.

The first quote I read from Ted Williams was that it wasn't his trade, it was Bob Short's trade. Well, let me say this: Bob Short, who owned the Senators, is a great guy and a fine sportsman and has more class on the tip of one finger than Williams has in his whole body.

How's a quote like that supposed to make me feel?

Here I am, coming off a 3–5 season in which I've been suspended and reinstated like a jack-in-the-box. I'm trying to get my career and my life back on the right track, with a fresh start, and my new manager disavows the trade. That's just beautiful. Really made me feel welcome.

At the first press conference, everything went fairly well and everybody said all the right things.

Then we chatted, one-to-one, and he gave me that bullshit comment about pitchers being dumb. He asked me how I like to pitch, and I told him that I'd always liked to pitch every fourth day.

"No way," said Teddy Ballgame. "I like to have my pitchers work every fifth day."

All I could say in response was that I had won 117 games and lost only 62 in the major leagues before I came under the expert guidance of one of the game's great hitting experts. You can't take a thing away from Ted Williams as a player. I respect him for all the great things he did on the playing field, and don't care a damn how he treated the fans or the Boston press. He was very likely one of the greatest hitters ever to pull on a pair of spikes.

As a manager and as a handler of men, he stank.

We didn't resolve the pitching rotation business then, but decided to discuss it further when we got to spring training.

Despite the early confrontation, I was anxious to get to Pompano Beach, Florida, to begin a new season. For all practical purposes, I had been out for a whole year and I had all the

0

enthusiasm of a rookie. At the same time, I was a veteran, and I figured I knew how to pace myself to get in shape.

And I pitched well in spring training, and he let me pitch every fourth day. I had a little flare-up with inflammation in my shoulder, but I hurried up to my doctor in Lakeland and got a shot of cortisone and was better in a hurry.

It seemed Williams and I were developing a pretty good rapport. Again, both of us were saying all the right things. Curt Flood came to camp after being out of baseball and Williams made a statement to newsmen that it was good to have some other notable and quotable people on the club. I guess he was trying to sound modest, and that ain't easy for Theodore Samuel.

But the club had confidence, we acquired Tom McCraw, and everybody seemed happy.

Dick Bosman got the opening day assignment and that was only fair, since he had pitched well the season before. We won the opener 8–0, then Dave McNally beat us 3–2 even though we played well. We weren't making any of those stupid mental errors.

My big night was April 9 and it had been ballyhooed for weeks. They pulled about 27,000 fans for the game and I managed to beat the Yankees 5–4 in ten innings. The Red Sox beat me next time out.

Williams immediately put me on a five-day rotation. His explanation then was that we had an off day, and he wanted to look at some other pitchers. Fine. I beat Cleveland 4–0.

Under "my" system, my next start would have been Thursday. But that was an off day, so I started Friday night against Milwaukee and had a no-hitter for five innings, but wound up losing the game. In my next start I shut out the Twins 2–0 and I was throwing the baseball very, very well indeed.

And the club was still playing well. We came off the road with a 12–8 record and everyone was excited about our chances.

The White Sox whacked us four in a row, our hitting stopped, and Williams panicked. He started going platoon crazy. Everyone's confidence was shot, mainly his. I pitched in Milwaukee, had a 3–2 lead and had to come out in the seventh inning when I developed a kink in my back with two runners on base. Our relief pitchers couldn't get the side out and I wound up losing.

117

O

The following Sunday in Minnesota the Twins got me 5–4 in ten innings.

A couple of days later, we were bogged down in an eight- or nine-game losing streak and Williams decided to call a workout at ten in the morning. And we had to play a game later that night!

I wasn't the only player who was upset. All twenty-five players on the roster were pissed. We decided to go to the workout, but we'd go on our own instead of on the team bus from the hotel. The bus left, with just Williams and the coaches on board. All we wanted to do was to show Williams that we were together, and that as a group we were sick and tired of his concepts about pitching and platooning and just about everything else having to do with managing a major league team.

Williams was seething. For a couple of days, he went around like a wild ship captain looking for the culprit who stole his strawberries. Ted wanted to know who organized the bus boycott.

I'd always heard Ted Williams was unique, but for the rest of the year he was eerie. And the more he ranted, the more ineffective we became.

I beat my old Detroit teammates 3–2 before some twenty thousand at RFK Stadium, but next time out Sam McDowell gave us nothing but bee-bees. Then we moved to Detroit for a four-game series. We got shut out Friday night, Bosman got beat 3–1 on Saturday, my old friend Mickey Lolich pitched a helluva game and beat me 4–0 in the opener on Sunday, then someone else goose-egged us in the second game. Three shutouts in four games. Things were very sad.

In the nightcap, Williams called on Don Mincher to pinch hit and Mincher didn't hear him right away. So Williams began bellowing at him and from that day on Mincher was in his doghouse. Just because he didn't snap to when the commander-in-chief spoke. Mincher was ready to quit and so was Tim Cullen. After that series, Cullen threw his spikes all the way across the locker room and said, "There's just no way I can play for this man."

The Senators had just stopped hitting and, without runs, God himself can get no better than a scoreless tie. My record was 4–6 when Williams decided his method of pitching every five days would be put into effect.

By late June, I couldn't keep my mouth shut. We were dropping fly balls, missing the cutoff man, failing to bunt—you name it—and I was losing close games one after another. Mel Stottlemyre of the Yankees shut us out 3–0 and Williams jerked me out of the game. So I barked.

"I don't want to pitch here anymore."

"God damn it, McLain, you're not going to decide when and where you pitch, and furthermore you're not going to yell at me."

I apologized to him after the game, but we were to have other battles, and bigger ones.

In July my shoulder was hurting so much I went on the disabled list for twenty-one days. They may have been the most pleasant days of the season. Williams had taken all the fire out of me. I was almost totally defeated and I was at a point where I hated to go to the park.

Later on, I didn't care what I said, or who heard me. One evening on the bench one of our players, Dick Billings, was talking about hitting and he made a comment to the effect that "just because you read a medical book, that doesn't make you a good surgeon." He never got the rest of the words out. Williams began glaring at him and muttering. Williams, and everyone else, knew the analogy Billings was drawing. Williams, the great hitter, couldn't manage for shit.

But he surely could swear. He cut loose on Billings and called him every name in the book, accusing him of not utilizing his full ability, and so on. Finally I butted in. Leave it to me.

"Ted, you fail to realize that you had so much ability that you can't overlook the shortcomings of a normal player."

Somehow, I don't think my comments made any impression at all on him.

Not long after that, he yanked me in the third inning in a game against Cleveland and I blew up at him. We went round and round in his office, and finally he threw me out, told me he hated my guts and that it'd be best to sever our relationship.

I talked to Short and all he wanted to do was keep the peace. I honestly believe Williams had him so buffaloed that Short rued the day he ever hired him.

Williams had an obsession about Carl Yastrzemski. I think down deep inside he hated Yaz. I know he wanted to show Yaz up every time we played the Red Sox, particularly in Boston. If the situation demanded that Yaz be walked with men on base, Williams would insist that his man pitch to Yaz to try to embarrass him by getting him out with men in scoring position.

We lost more games to the Red Sox because of Williams

trying to satisfy his own ego. Maybe he wanted Yaz to look bad so not a single Boston Red Sox fan would ever forget how great Teddy Ballgame was when he played for that team.

Williams had a hard and fast rule against playing golf.

"It's a thousand bucks' fine if I even *think* you're playing golf."

That was his warning.

So four of us formed a group, called ourselves The Touring Pros, and played every damned day on the road. Our baseball was so pitiful the golf couldn't hurt it.

Williams never got a dime from me, or from anyone else in the foursome so far as I know.

I guess when the Yankees had those great teams, the writers used to say that the managers didn't really manage at all, and that things went along so smoothly that sometimes the manager would have to be awakened on the bench when the game was over.

Today's managers are inclined to overmanage, and Williams was the worst offender. He'd order a guy with a pretty good fast ball to stick to the slider and curve. He had Don Mincher sitting on the bench for weeks against pitchers everyone else knew Mincher could handle.

When Curt Flood joined the club, he was really anxious to play. When he got off to a slow start—understandable because of his layoff—Williams made up his mind Curt needed to be platooned. And that hurt Curt more than anything.

I know, because our lockers were adjoining, and we had many conversations about Williams the egomaniac. I'm certain Ted Williams drove Curt Flood out of baseball. Here's a guy making $100,000 a year and he walks away from it, all because one man makes up his mind that another man can't hit.

I'm convinced that Ted Williams got up every day and had to remind himself that he really was the boss of twenty-five athletes. Then he reminded us. Things like not letting us stay at our homes in the Washington area when we were playing in Baltimore, just thirty miles down the road.

When Darold Knowles and Mike Epstein were traded to Oakland, Short asked Knowles what was wrong with the Senators, and Knowles told him, "Mr. Short, you're not going to like this, but the problem with this team is Ted Williams."

After Bernie Allen was traded to the Yankees, he told reporters about his confrontation with Williams. It happened in late July.

0

Williams: "How are you?"

Allen: "I'd be better if I were playing more."

Bernie said the Great One never spoke to him the rest of the season, and after he was traded away Allen never spoke to Williams when they'd meet at the park. "He doesn't like me," said Bernie, "and I don't like him. What's the use pretending?"

If there was a man on the team who liked Ted Williams, I don't know his name. Joe Coleman, who went to Detroit in the deal that sent me to Washington, had some unkind things to say about Williams. Allen called Williams, "Probably the most egotistical man I've ever met in my life."

Williams loved to verbally kick the shit out of players in front of other players, or the press. Harassment was his game. I don't think he considered it a good day unless he publicly humiliated someone.

When he sent Jim French to the minor leagues, he made it as painful as possible for Jim.

One night not long before Frenchie was sent down, I asked Williams for a change in catchers. I didn't have anything against Paul Casanova—except that he frequently threw the ball back to me harder than I threw it to him—but my luck was sour and I thought a change might be good.

Frenchie caught and we lost anyway, but Williams couldn't understand the whole thing. He thought it was a friendship deal. As long as I played the game, I've never let friendship interfere with my desire to win.

When Williams told French he was being sent down to the Denver farm club, Frenchie asked Ted if his being farmed out had anything to do with me. Well, Ted lit into him, accused him of being one of the organizers of the bus boycott and made all sorts of wild comments that were totally unnecessary. He accused French of trying to undermine his authority.

No one needed to undermine Ted Williams. He was doing a total job of it, all by himself.

The pitchers got together and formed a club and we imposed fines for such things as walking the opposing pitcher, failure to back up the play, not moving a man along, or not running full out. It didn't amount to much, but it was fun and it was good for the morale of the club.

But Williams made it clear he didn't like that idea, and we stopped the meetings, simply because we were intimidated.

Ted Williams made the game of baseball quit being fun.

O

He told a writer, "Half this club is over the hill and the other half isn't ready for the big leagues."

That does a lot for the confidence of a team, seeing a quote like that.

Williams got the players so frustrated they had to laugh to keep from going crazy. He kept talking about people trying to undermine his authority. That was one of his favorite terms.

There are four stalls in the back bathroom of the Senators' locker room and one day there were names scrawled inside the stalls: Number one, Bernie Allen; number two, Denny McLain; number three, Tommy McCraw, and number four, a tie between Dick Billings and Tim Cullen. It was the joke of the year. "The Underminers" had been born officially, and I don't know to this day who put the names up there. But we took great pride in our ratings, and before long the "klan" was growing.

We were the people dedicated (in our minds anyway) to the overthrow of Ted Williams. Since Bernie Allen's name was in the first shithouse stall, he was crowned Imperial Wizard of the Underminers.

One night we had a big party for the players, and some of us dressed up in sheets and inducted six new members. We carried crosses and everything, and made the inductees give reasons why they felt they deserved to be in the group. Toby Harrah had the funniest reply: "Because I'm the youngest utility player in the major leagues."

Fun was hard to come by when Ted Williams was managing so you had to go out and create it, however you could.

Williams treated Tim Cullen brutally. Tim just wasn't blessed with a great deal of hitting ability, but no one tried harder. Time after time he'd consult with Williams in an effort to improve himself.

Late in the 1971 season, Williams walked up to Timmy in the training room at Oakland and told Tim he should quit baseball because his career was behind him. Now if that's any way to talk to a major league ballplayer I'll kiss your bippy. Williams totally demoralized an entire team.

Toby Harrah is playing excellent baseball now for the Texas Rangers, but if he had to contend with Williams any longer, the Great One might have ruined him, too. Harrah was fulfilling an obligation to the armed services and was commuting to the ball park every night for two weeks while he was in summer camp. Williams not only didn't let him play (and Toby had been hitting the ball well, too) but nicknamed him Sleepy.

0

Elliott Maddox managed to play regularly for the Yankees, but he couldn't play for Williams. Even when he's trying to be funny, Williams winds up being sarcastic.

One night he asked Maddox, "Do you think we could take a chance on you for defensive play?"

Elliott assured Williams he could do the job, but Williams wasn't through. He had to get another shot in at Elliott.

"Too bad you can't hit."

That was enough for Maddox, so he shot back, "It's pretty hard to hit from the bench where I spend all my time."

Davey Nelson wasn't the greatest defensive infielder in the history of our national pastime but Williams found a way to make his criticism anything but constructive.

"Get a couple of mattresses, and this winter spend all your spare time diving on them. Put one on your left and one on your right."

That's Teddy Boy. Had to make a big issue out of it in front of people, in order to humiliate another human being. He's the coldest, cruelest man I've ever met.

No wonder lots of people always call him the Kid.

He just never quite grew up.

Maybe playing for one season under Ted Williams made me appreciate Mayo Smith even more. Mayo and I were together four full seasons—well, one of them wasn't very full—longer than any other manager I played for.

Frankly, the first year Mayo and I didn't get along. I was a cocky kid just blossoming into whatever I was blossoming into, and he was a guy who'd been around and seen lots of cocky kids. We clashed right away, then stayed pretty much away from each other.

We had that falling out at the end of the 1967 season, and I still maintain that had it not been for Mayo's surliness and my stupidity, the Tigers would have won the pennant a year earlier than they did.

In 1968 nobody could have handled the Tigers any better than Mayo did. We had a bunch of guys who couldn't run, who couldn't throw anybody out, who couldn't bunt, who couldn't hit behind the runner. What you had to do was sit on your fanny and wait for the guys to hit.

Mayo knew his talent, and he was a patient man. I think maybe a younger manager would have panicked somewhere along the line, but Mayo never did. The Tiger fans never once really warmed up to him, and I'd bet if you poll them today they'd rate him as a mediocre manager. The fact is, he did a superb job.

When I first broke into organized baseball in 1962, I was with the Harlan, Kentucky, club for just two games. It was a combined White Sox-Yankee team in a rookie league and as I recall there were two managers, but I wasn't there long enough to remember them.

Ira Hutchinson had me under his wing at Clinton, Iowa, later that year. He was a nice, friendly man who tried his best to teach me how to throw a curve ball. He had me pitching every day, either in a game or in the bullpen, working on a curve that just couldn't happen.

Ira was probably the best security guard baseball has ever known. Every time I tried to sneak across that bridge to go back to Illinois to see my girl, Ira knew about it.

Bobby Mavis was our manager with the Duluth-Superior club of the Northern League. He really didn't have to do any managing and I don't know what his capabilities might have been. We just had outstandingly good talent and we ran away with the competition. But Mavis was a feisty little guy who had a sort of plastic air about him. I never really got to know him, and it never bothered me that I didn't. He never trusted me and Jim Rooker, always thought we were out running around. I know it doesn't sound too modest, but isn't it strange, the club's best pitcher and its best hitter getting the most bullshit from the manager?

We won seventy-seven and lost only forty-three and I had a 13–2 record and our pitching staff set a record with seventy-five complete games. Now, how much more can a manager want than that? And Rookie was knocking down every fence in the league.

I had Frank Carswell a couple of times as a manager, at Knoxville in '63 and at Syracuse briefly in '64. He was a dandy guy who never quite made it in the big leagues, but he had a big league attitude and the players liked him. I always thought he'd have made a pretty good major league manager, but then my judgment on managers has never been sought.

My great fondness for Charlie Dressen is well known. It's only natural that I'd have a good feeling for the guy who brought me to the major leagues; but more than that, Charlie was a great teacher and a scrappy guy who knew a lot of base-ball and knew how to appraise his talent. He may have had to

O

say things to appease fans and writers once in a while, but he knew where the talent was, and how to use it. Of course, Charlie had a fine reputation for working with young pitchers, and I couldn't count the hours he spent with me, teaching me how to throw a curve ball, talking to me about setting up hitters and utilizing my skills.

Maybe Charlie represented some sort of father-image to me, I don't know. I didn't have a father then, and I was only nineteen, and I know our relationship was a little deeper than the normal one between player and manager.

Charlie was a great psychologist, even though he didn't have a lot of formal education.

Two other guys taught me some pretty good lessons about pitching, too. There's always been a lot of controversy about Johnny Sain, but he worked like hell with me on my slider and got my thinking straightened around.

And Bob Swift was a helluva man when he managed in the minors and when he coached for Charlie. Mechanically, he didn't know a thing about the science of pitching. But he had been a catcher, and he had caught some dandy pitchers in his time, and he knew the psychology of pitching. He taught me several things. One, never change-up when you're ahead of a hitter. Only do it when you're even or behind him.

And Swift believed in sticking with your best stuff. If you're a fast ball pitcher, and your fast ball is alive, then keep throwing it until they get two hits in a row off you. He kept beating that into me when he managed our Mayaguez club in the Puerto Rican League, and it stuck with me all through my career.

Swift was interim manager of the Tigers when Charlie Dressen first became ill; then they both died in 1966, Dressen of heart trouble and Swift of cancer. I reckon the noble thing to do is to say what a great manager Swift was, but once he got into that major league seat, he turned into a horse's ass.

Although to a much lesser extent than Williams, Swift nevertheless reminded you all the time that he was the boss, and that he was calling the shots.

It occurs to me that if a man has authority, he really isn't compelled to go around yelling about it all the time, unless he's trying to convince himself.

The man who succeeded Swift after he fell ill doesn't even deserve a mention. His name is Frank Skaff, and he's been with the Tiger organization a thousand years, mostly as a scout. As

0

for his scouting, I would compare Frank Skaff with the corporal who told Custer, "C'mon, George, there ain't no Indians over that hill."

As a major league manager, well, Skaff simply wasn't one. He was in way over his head and had no credentials for the job. They just needed a body to throw in there and his was the closest to the man doing the throwing. Skaff shouldn't be allowed in the ball park even if he paid for his own ticket.

He gave me my most embarrassing moment in baseball, and I'll never forgive him for it. One of the Detroit writers quoted me as describing the Tigers as a "country-club set" with a don't-give-a-shit attitude.

Skaff never bothered to check it out with me to see if I had been misquoted (and I had been). Instead, he instantly called a clubhouse meeting, and in front of twenty-four other players, gave me one of the severest verbal ass-whippings I've ever had. I didn't appreciate it then, and every time I think about it now, years later, I appreciate it even less.

As I was tumbling down the major league ladder, I encountered three other managers—Dick Williams, Luman Harris, and Eddie Mathews.

The difference between Dick Williams and Ted Williams is that Dick has a very good understanding of the game, and he's a very good manager. However, he's not quite as good as he thinks he is. He'd get a couple of snorts in him and he'd start yapping about how he didn't have to take all this crap from Charlie Finley, that he had offers from half a dozen other major league teams. It occurred to me at the time that the Oakland Athletics of that vintage could pretty well manage themselves.

I thought it was a sign of immaturity that Williams had a penchant for ripping his players in the press. But in Oakland, it's not uncommon for the players to rip back in exactly the same way. In the final analysis, however, Williams knew what he had going for him, he didn't bog things down with a lot of silly rules, and all he really expected was a sharp performance on the field. Most all the time, the A's gave that to him.

Luman Harris was the manager of the Atlanta Braves when they rescued me after a brief stint in Birmingham. I had gone there after being cut loose by the A's, and much as I disliked being in the minor leagues again, it was nice playing under a classy guy like Phil Cavaretta. But that lasted just a few weeks.

And I never really got to know Luman Harris, either. The Braves fired him right after I arrived in Atlanta. But I really liked the guy. Maybe that's why they fired him, figuring if McLain likes him, he must be a dumb shit.

Harris was succeeded by Eddie Mathews and therein lies a strange turn of events. I had played briefly with Mathews during the 1968 season when the Tigers acquired him late in the season. Like a lot of players at the tail end of their careers, Mathews liked to get into the sauce now and again. But he was a decent guy.

He was coaching the Braves when I got there, and he couldn't have been friendlier. But the minute he became the manager, he did a complete flip-flop. He started with that dictator shit and became unbearable. The guys on the club all had the same reaction I did: Okay, so we're not the greatest team in the world, but why do we have to take all this garbage?

It didn't take the Atlanta organization long to figure out that there was one helluva difference between Eddie Mathews the third baseman and hitting star, and Eddie Mathews the manager. The one did his job and did it well. The other was a flop.

I said at the outset that a manager's job is not an easy one. As a matter of reality, it's a most difficult and lonely one. He never quite knows how friendly to be with his players. He's dealing with twenty-five different personalities, with some guys who need to be kicked in the hind end and with others who need coddling.

If his team wins, the players get all the credit. If the team loses, the manager gets fired. He may be named manager of the year along the line, but if he leaves a pitcher in one pitch too long, the fans are on his ass like the green on grass.

For sure, a manager cannot understand everything about his players, their little quirks, what makes them tick or quit ticking; and some managers I've known really didn't try very hard to understand.

But lots of players never stop to think about a manager's difficulties. I know. For a few years, I was a player myself.

DOWNHILL

8

ALL THE WAY

Being in the minor leagues isn't bad if you're on the way up. Matter of fact, it's not half-bad.

Being there when you're on your way down is a bummer.

The difference can't be measured just in money. It's not just a whole new ball game, it's another way of life. It's particularly difficult when you have a gut feeling that you're never going back up the ladder again.

The difference then is about three million light years.

Once I hit the minor leagues for the second time in my career, I think I knew—in those occasional moments when I was compelled to be honest with Denny McLain—that the only trip I'd take from then on was on a smoky bus.

God, how I tried to lie to myself. I kidded myself that the fast ball was coming back and that the pain was going away. I was tempted to look at my birth certificate to make certain I was only twenty-eight years old. My arm seemed so much older. My brain? Who the hell knows. So much had happened it seemed I had lived a hundred lives.

One evening, as my coauthor and I were sitting around putting together things for this book, he read me a quote that I've had a hard time forgetting: "He who lives more lives than one, more deaths than one must die."

I'm not sure who said it, but he must have been through some kind of hell himself.

When I started downhill, I didn't even know it.

I had been on the skids for three years before I forced a bit of candor down my own throat and became painfully aware of what was happening to my professional life.

They say statistics don't lie and that they're for losers. Whatever else they are, they're good for a while if a fellow wants to bullshit himself.

A good pitcher who wins a lot of games but whose earned run average doesn't sparkle will tell you, and anyone else who'll listen, that earned run averages are deceiving. If his ERA is good and the won-lost figures not too impressive, he'll insist the ERA is everything.

The year I won thirty-one games, I struck out 280 batters. The following season I won twenty-four and fanned a hundred fewer batters. The ERA had risen about one run every nine innings.

But when you're on the skids, you tell yourself little things like that don't matter. Sometimes, if there's no one else around, you can begin to believe the little lies you tell yourself.

0

Because of the three suspensions and all the other trouble, I persuaded myself that the 1970 season just didn't happen. It happened, all right, but it was a bad dream, a cancerous sort of thing that had been cut out of my system. By the time I went to spring training with the Senators, I felt in my heart I could be a big winner again. Let's not kid ourselves—I had no conception of winning thirty-one games again. Like I said before, there's no way in the world I even wanted to live that kind of season over again.

Every failure has to be blamed on someone, so I conveniently put the responsibility for my 1971 miseries on Ted Williams and teammates who, while nice folks and good buddies, were not destined for Cooperstown. Just because I won 31 percent of my games after having won 83 percent just three seasons before didn't mean the talent had suddenly gone out of me.

Even today, when I can look at things more honestly, I realize that while some of my velocity had disappeared, some of my poor showing in Washington *can* be traced directly to Williams. He had me so whipped mentally that all I wanted was out.

Although I made some good friends in Washington, there was no way I would have returned to that club as long as Ted Williams was going to manage. In the off season the franchise was moved to Arlington, Texas, and Williams was hired to stay as manager. Only my faith in Short, that he would trade me, persuaded me to go to spring training again.

It happened early in spring training. Twice I had been canceled out when I was scheduled to pitch, and that's always a tipoff when a trade is imminent. Short came to me and said, "Denny, I have great news for you."

He could have told me I was going to the Rhode Island Reds of the Chicken League and I'd have kissed him.

Good news, my ass. It was great news. He told me I was going to Oakland. Beautiful. Not only am I escaping a bad team and a horrible manager, but I'm going to a fine team.

The deal was McLain for Jim Panther and Don Stanhouse. When you're traded for two guys with so little talent between them, that's another sign you're not a superstar any longer. The only thing more disruptive to one's confidence is to be traded "for a player to be named later."

That, my friends, is one of the signs that you are definitely washed up.

I wasn't. Not quite.

0

I hurried to the Oakland camp and met the genius, Dick Williams. There was the customary rah-rah stuff, glad to have you here and all that. Everyone figured I'd take Vida Blue's place in the starting rotation since he was having his much-publicized hassle with Charlie Finley, and I believed it, too.

Reggie Jackson showed up for the press conference. Reggie always showed up when there were cameras present.

I knew I could still pitch and could still win. It was exciting to be with a good, solid team again. I just knew I'd be in the World Series.

Matter of fact, I was so certain of it that Ken Holtzman and I went to Las Vegas a few days later and I blew the World Series check I never got.

First time out in spring training I got bombed by Milwaukee. The ball carried a mile. Naturally I blamed it on the dry air in Arizona.

The next couple of times out things were better; then one day Williams let me go six or seven innings against San Diego and I must have given up ten runs. They were hitting rockets like they were coming off the launching pad at Cape Kennedy.

"How do you feel?" Williams wanted to know.

"Hell, don't ask me. Ask the outfielders. They're taking all the punishment."

Things weren't that bad later on. We had the brief player strike, and that set me back just at a time when I was getting into shape. I lasted five games, won one and lost a pair, and then I was out in the cold. Williams gave me the news after a Sunday game.

"Look, Charlie is trying to make a deal and we're gonna have to send you out. Why don't you go to Des Moines?"

No way. No fucking way at all. Suddenly I realized I was just a fill-in until Vida decided to play the game. He and Finley made their deal, then Finley put the screws to me.

Since it was after the May 15 cutdown date, he had to pay me for the entire year. The cheap bastard wanted to make a settlement. He offered me $25,000 and my moving expenses. For the rest of the year he'd have had to pay me $45,000. I told him I'd take the $25,000 if he paid the taxes on it. Charlie agreed, and said there'd be a news conference tomorrow.

The next morning, an hour or so before the scheduled news conference, Finley informed me he'd give me the $25,000 but the tax deal was off. I told him right then and there the

0

whole deal was off. Instead of taking the payoff and getting out of baseball, I'd go to the minor leagues just to keep from getting screwed financially.

So the next stop was Birmingham, Alabama.

Chuck Dobson met my plane and we sat up and talked until five thirty the next morning. Chuck and I became good friends. Ironically, he had been the opposing pitcher the day I won my thirtieth game, and he was in Birmingham to try and pitch himself back to the majors, too, after an arm operation.

The manager was Phil Cavaretta, one of my boyhood idols, and I had just enough vodka in me to roust him out of bed so he could officially welcome me to the Birmingham baseball team. Phil was always a classy guy and he wasn't upset. Maybe he was as disappointed about managing in the bush leagues as I was about pitching there.

I stayed just a few weeks, pitched in eight games, was involved in six decisions and won half of them. In the later games, I was throwing the ball pretty well. One of the games I pitched in Birmingham was surely one of the quickest in baseball history.

Sharyn was pregnant with our fourth child, Michelle, so she had stayed back at our home in Walnut Creek, California. I was scheduled to pitch the next afternoon when I got a call from Holtzman.

"Sharyn's gonna deliver early and I wanna know what to do."

"What the hell do you mean, what do you do? You idiot, you take her to the hospital."

At that time of night, I couldn't get a flight out. Even if there were a plane, I couldn't possibly get there in time for the delivery. Cavaretta had told me major league scouts were watching me, so I made the decision to pitch the next day, then hurry to California.

It was a seven-inning game. I finished things up in an hour and nine minutes and lost 2–1 then got on the first thing smoking westward.

As it turned out, both Sharyn and the baby were fine, but Holtzman was a wreck. He had taken my wife to the hospital and paced the floor so much everyone thought he was the expectant father. When she got back to the room, Holtzman hurried in to see her. "How the fuck do you feel?"

That's my man, Kenny. Just can't keep that word out of his

vocabulary and uses it anytime, in front of anyone. And I love him, because he's a beautifully kind and considerate human being.

A month later I was back in the major leagues. Eddie Robinson called me and said, "I want to welcome you to the Atlanta Braves."

The deal was for Orlando Cepeda.

At least this time I was involved in a trade with a major league player. Somehow, I sensed this was absolutely my last chance in the big leagues.

I was with the club just four days before I got a chance to pitch. It was Fourth of July night in Atlanta Stadium and the event had been properly promoted. They got 50,597 into the park and I was to pitch the second game. I knew damn good and well where the crowd came from and I was in a beautiful frame of mind for the big event.

The crowd gave me a standing ovation when I went out to pitch. All Luman Harris did was give me the baseball and say, "Just do a job, Denny. I have confidence in you."

I did the job, but I did it too quickly. I went seven innings before the rains came. We were leading Houston and I was pitching too quickly, trying to get things done to beat the rain. But the Cubs got a couple of runs off me and tied the game 3–3 and the deluge came.

It was a long way from winning thirty-one, but it beat the hell out of Birmingham.

But the Braves didn't, not by much. They were having their troubles, the pitching wasn't good and there was a lot of front office disenchantment with Luman Harris as manager. That figured. Any guy I liked would be sure to be in a lot of deep shit.

Luman asked me to go to the bullpen since the Braves wanted to look at some other pitchers as potential starters. He said they pretty much knew what I could do.

Funny, I took that as a compliment. Amazing what your mind will do for you when you're looking under rocks for assurance.

So I went to the bullpen, with Luman assuring me that if I did well, I'd be counted on heavily in 1973. I was—in Des Moines and Shreveport; and Luman was out of a job a few days after I went to the bullpen.

Eddie Mathews, whom I had met in '68 when he played briefly for the Tigers, became the manager. He had been a big hero for the Braves as a player, but up to the time he was

0

named manager he was serving as first base coach. Ordinarily, first base coaches are lucky if they can keep track of the outs.

When he was winding down as a player, Mathews had a crappy attitude, as lots of older players do. They're resentful of the younger guys, and everything they see looks like horseshit to them.

When Mathews took over as manager, he donned his Nazi attitude and started barking out orders to a team that had a pretty casual attitude about everything. He was particularly caustic to me, didn't use me much, but told me I figured in his plans for the following year. Right on, Eddie. His plan was for me to be out on my ass.

Over the winter I agreed to take a cut in pay from $75,000 to $50,000. I had a choice, since the cut was larger than the trimming permitted under baseball rules. My alternative was to get an unconditional release.

Spring training was uneventful. The Braves still weren't going anywhere and everyone knew it except the front office. Of course, front offices keep hoping for miracles.

Sharyn had filed divorce papers the previous summer, after Michelle was born, but we quickly got back together and I wanted the family with me during spring training. While we looked for suitable housing, we stayed in a hotel. I had arranged to pay the bill twice a month. We were staying in a suite and I guess the manager got panicky and insisted on having some money ahead of time.

"Don't sweat, you'll get your money."

He did sweat, enough to call Donald Davidson, the right-hand man to the Braves' chairman of the board, and accuse me of using abusive language.

Abusive language? Maybe I told him to go fuck himself, but I don't think that's too abusive.

Now, when Davidson came to me yelling and screaming about the reputation of the ball club being at stake, and bringing up the old skeletons about my past financial problems, I surely did become abusive with Davidson. I had some serious questions about his ancestry, his gender, and his sexual habits.

A week later I was packing again. I got the hint from Lew Burdette, Mathews's pitching coach. I asked him what innings I'd be pitching that night and he said he wasn't sure and that I should talk with Mathews.

For Burdette to profess uncertainty about anything was unthinkable. Here's a pitching coach who could teach a pitcher little except a spitball, and he doesn't know when I'm pitching.

Burdette and I didn't get along anyway. Rule one with Lew was that in order to get along with him, you had to kiss ass, and I've never developed an appetite for that.

So I went to Mathews, and there was no hesitation on his part.

"I have some bad news for you," he stammered. "We're giving you your outright release."

Naturally I wanted to know why. I had been pitching pretty well.

"Well, some situations have come up that I have no control over. Now, I think you can still pitch. I know you can pitch. But not here."

I had my answer. Then Eddie Robinson came in and wanted to know when I'd be leaving.

"The minute I can get my shit out of that fucking door, Mr. Robinson."

The politics of baseball was grabbing me by the throat and trying to choke the life out of me. But I was almost to the point of not caring by then. I had some businesses going in Atlanta, my family had already gone back there, and I was prepared to turn my back on baseball forever. I didn't want to play. I went home, and didn't make a single call to a single major league club. All I could think of was, "Thank God, it's over."

I had had it with baseball and there was plenty of evidence that baseball had had it with me.

I decided to give the business world another chance to eat me alive. Besides, now I could play golf every day.

So that was my schedule for a couple of months, until Ray Johnson called from Des Moines. He not only called once, he called a dozen times, begging me to come back to baseball. Finally I agreed to fly up and have lunch with him, and to at least talk things over. I liked him immediately.

He offered me $2,000 a month, $10,000 if I was picked up by a major league club, and we agreed to split everything above $10,000. He knew I could put people in the park, but I don't believe to this day that was Ray's main reason for hiring me. He said, "Denny, all I want is to see you back in the big leagues." I'm convinced he meant every word of that.

I bought the deal. First guys I ran into with the club were Joe Keough and Tom Egan and I thought, "Hell, the worst this can be is a good time."

0

I tinkered around for a couple of weeks trying to get in shape. I guess it was twenty days before I pitched, and I went six innings. Baseball was fun again. Sharyn and the kids came to Des Moines and we had a super time until July and I was freezing my ass off. I told Ray I was in shape, but not in what you'd call pitching shape. He asked if I'd prefer the climate in Shreveport. He owned that club, too, so we decided to pack up and leave again.

Here's a guy who was going out of his way to be nice to me. Even when my wife and kids were back in Atlanta, he'd pay for me to fly back to visit my family between starts. Can a man get any more considerate than that?

He made the whole summer a vacation for us.

I'm just sorry I didn't pitch better for him—and, naturally, for myself.

But, nobody's perfect. Right?

The only difficulty I had in Des Moines was with the manager of the club, Joe Sparks. He told me on the phone, before I ever joined the club, "Now, Denny, I don't want any trouble from you."

Well, that's a horseshit attitude for anyone to take, and I let him know it. Who's he to go telling me about trouble? He doesn't know what trouble is.

We had precious little of it, he and I, once we started playing ball. I spent lots of time playing golf and betting the ponies every time we got near a track. Once, at a track near Omaha, one of our friends had some lock-city information. Some of those can't-lose ponies.

I bet a hundred to win and two hundred to place and show and the horse wins from here to Antiquity, Ohio. I was $2,500 up. Our next hot tip was in the eighth race but we couldn't stay because we had to get back for a night game.

I put half my winnings on the thing and he's still running today.

The other two hot flashes were going the following day, but we had a day game. We were praying for a fast game. It figured. Ball game starts at one-thirty. First race is at three-thirty. Our nag is in the third race and if we make it to the track by four-thirty we'll win a fortune. The game went thirteen innings, we sped to the track in time to see our horse going across the finish line with everything else trailing. There went $11,000 down the drain.

Hell, that would have financed a weekend in Vegas!

0

But we still had one tip to go, in the ninth race. The nag ran well, but didn't win. It seems that's the way everything was going for me about that time.

Perhaps at about this time I began to look around and see people and things as they really were. We had some crazy kids on that club, kids who had no idea what the major leagues were all about, who had only a dream, as I once had. It was different for me. I knew the taste of that success, and I wanted it back. I knew what I was missing. They didn't.

On to Shreveport. The manager there was the former major league infielder, Gene Freese. He'd been through some distressing personal problems and he had an Olympic-sized hard-on for the world. Since I was still officially a part of the world, at least on a part-time basis, I was included in his group of things to despise.

Nobody liked him. There was no reason for me to be different. First time I met him he gave me the tired old managerial line about, "We have rules and regulations and everybody has to follow them, including you, McLain. You'll be treated like everyone else."

Hell, the Shreveport team was only 174 games out of first place, so it either had no talent or he was treating them wrong. No one talked to Freese. In a sense, I felt sorry for him.

There were lots of reasons why we should have gotten along. We both had been in the major leagues. We both wanted to get back as quickly as possible. We had both endured some heavy personal problems.

You think I wanted to spend the rest of my life with the Shreveport club? There was an awful stench in the clubhouse. All you could smell was the urinal. The floors were made out of cement. When the hot water worked, it was rusty. The clothes had to be hung on hooks.

The weather was God-awful hot and muggy, but that's what I wanted so I could get my arm in shape. The pain at this time was almost unbearable but somehow I still hoped for a miracle.

When I walked into Freese's office, I told him I'd do whatever he asked and would help with the pitching staff if he needed me. If I could no longer throw the ball past the good hitters, I at least could teach those kids something about the art of pitching. And that was it. I walked out onto the field and started talking with some of the kids. I left my shirt in the clubhouse and wore just my sweatshirt (and my pants, of course).

O

I wasn't there fifteen minutes when Freese yelled out:

"If you'd be so kind, superstar, it'd be nice if you'd put your shirt on. After all, there are people coming into this park."

Fuck him! I wasn't about to get pinched for indecent exposure. Besides, the people who were in that park were there to see me, not him.

"Of course, Mr. Stengel. I'll be right there."

So, for a time I ignored him. Then one night in Amarillo we sat down for a few drinks and ironed out all our problems. By the time I left Shreveport, I think we understood each other's frustrations.

I left a week or so before the season was over.

I left because it occurred to me that it was all over. Every damned bit of it. The good, the bad, the mediocre. It was all behind me.

I had pitched a game in Shreveport and two scouts from the Cincinnati Reds came to see me work. I had good stuff and I threw the shit out of the ball, but I was wild. I've never had control problems in my life, and here I was, trying to find the plate, walking guys, and running up the count on others.

Still, I struck out ten or twelve, and looked good as far as getting people out.

Would the scouts understand that? Couldn't they see I could still pitch effectively?

No, they couldn't see any of that. The Reds called up some kid instead.

When I peeled off the soggy uniform that night, amid the stench of the Shreveport urinals, I didn't know if I'd ever pitch again, but I had made up my mind to one thing: I'd never again pitch in the minor leagues.

And I lied to myself, saying that whatever happened I'd never look back.

The truth is, I look back almost every day.

But nobody's perfect.

HANGUPS I ADMIT (AND A FEW I STILL DENY HAVING)

9

Hangups? You figure them out. I know about a few of them, and they don't seem so abnormal to me, growing up as I did and meeting the challenges of my own life. They have been my very own challenges, and the easiest thing in the world is to figure out what you'd do if you were in someone else's spot. The hell of it is, I was in my own spot. And I had to do things as best I could, with whatever judgment and maturity, or lack of same, I had at that time. Hindsight is a wonderful thing. Most folks have twenty-twenty hindsight, and given time to do it all over again, I'd like to think I'd exercise better judgment lots of times.

As a kid, I went to Ascension Catholic grade school in Harvey, Illinois, and was taught by Dominican nuns. At least they tried to teach me.

We had to wear blue shirts and dark blue bow ties.

No one will ever know how I hated that tie!

It just didn't make sense that a kid had to wear a tie. What in the name of God did that have to do with learning?

Don't tell me—I already know. It's discipline, and discipline is learning.

I think we made the switch to those silly bow ties in the seventh grade. Before that we wore the long blue ties and they weren't all that bad, as ties go, and I wish they would.

It was the first or second week of school, September, still very warm outside. The tie had been choking the life out of me all day. The minute the final bell rang I headed for the stairs, and once there I jerked that silly-assed tie from my collar.

The first bell meant that in five minutes school would be out. The second bell allowed everyone to leave in a straight line, a strict, straight military line. The third bell, at five past three, meant you could break line and go.

When the second bell sounded my tie came off. Sister Mary Margaret ordered me to put it back on. I was at the head of the line, in order to be first out of school, and she spotted me.

By the time she gave me the orders and I protested mildly, the third and final bell rang. Now there was no way I would put that tie back on, especially since we were officially out of school.

"The tie goes back on," she barked, "or you go to the principal's office."

That did it. I heaved the tie right out the window.

It may be difficult for non-Catholics to understand, but in the span of, say, thirty seconds Sister Mary Margaret had the fear of God, the Virgin Mary, and a handful of saints boiling up inside me. I marched my squat little fanny down those stairs to begin the search for that little blue bow tie.

I might as well have been searching for the Hope diamond. The bow tie was nowhere to be found. It was either down a drain or in someone's pocket. I returned to the principal's office, by the ear, knowing the worst was yet to happen.

Naturally, the blabbermouths called my folks. I got several lectures from various nuns and school officials, a threat that I was about to be expelled, and a wonderfully warm trip home with Mom and Dad.

Once home, the real fireworks began. My father tanned my ass for what seemed to be ten minutes and the order was not to be misunderstood: You stay in school, the tie stays on, and we get no more upsetting calls from the nuns.

It was one of those deals I couldn't turn down.

My father, Tom McLain, was a great man. He didn't achieve greatness in the sense that one normally thinks of greatness, but he was great in my eyes. My first memory of him was when I was about six years old and I fell into a pit. I think they were putting in the well in back of the house we were building in Markham, and they had started the excavation. Some friends and I were running around and I tumbled into what seemed to me a tremendously deep gorge. I was splashing around and screaming my lungs out for help.

My dad rushed over, looked down at me splashing around in the mud and crying, and said, "Dennis, stand up."

I did. The water was only up to my knees.

I've never been a good swimmer, though. Mark Spitz has nothing to fear from Denny McLain. To this day, I'd have trouble swimming across your average-sized room.

He started me into baseball at about that time. I never have thought of him as a guy who "pushed" me into it, but he did want me to excel and to do my best. From the very first, I wanted to play shortstop all the time, because that was my idea of being in the middle of every game.

Early on, I played shortstop, did some catching, played first base and the outfield, and did quite a bit of pitching.

When I was eight or nine years old, my heart was set on being a shortstop and nothing else. But I've always had bad hands. Gracefully gliding into the hole, digging out a bad-hop grounder, and throwing the man out at first base sounds glamorous. Problem was, I never could do it, and he knew it! One time I played first base for six innings, and I made seven errors.

0

It got so bad the other team was deliberately swinging late just to try to hit the ball to me. In the last inning, I couldn't take it any longer and I broke down crying. I threw myself right on the ground and bawled my eyes out.

My dad took it much better than I did.

"Denny, you're not a first baseman. But you're a good hitter and you can throw the ball harder than anyone on the team. So quit worrying. All this means is that you're not destined to be a first baseman."

My father was a strong disciplinarian. He ruled with an iron hand and a big, black belt. My brother Timmy, who's two years younger than I, knew as well as I did that once my father spoke, there was no appeal.

My mother, Betty, was the boss in the family when it came to the little, everyday decisions. She was much more outspoken than my father and always had a pretty quick temper.

I was always very close to my father. Over the years I have become alienated from my mother at times, and from my brother as well. The basic problem between myself and Timmy is a problem I think exists in a lot of families when the older son does well, and everyone begins comparing the two sons. Timmy's problem was that he's always had to live in my shadow.

And he was a good athlete in his own right and had several opportunities to play pro ball. I'm sure he would have made it, too, had he not been hurt in a car wreck.

My dad had the same opportunities, but he didn't make it—and for quite another reason. The Chicago Cubs made him an offer—but so did my mother. Dad was asked to report to a minor league club. My mother made his options very clear: If you go off and play baseball, there'll be no marriage.

He never talked about it, but down deep inside I think he always regretted never having the chance to make it. He and my mother had a beautiful marriage and a good relationship, so he never made an issue out of what might have been.

He always was sorry he didn't go to school and get a better education, too, but his father had died very young and my dad had to get out and hustle and help make a living for the family and help take care of two younger brothers and a younger sister. My dad ruled that family, too, and helped keep the other kids in line. He had a lot of responsibility put on his shoulders at a very tender age.

College was out of the question for him. He wasn't long out

of high school when he had to go into service in World War II. Matter of fact, he was in Germany in combat when I was born.

When I started blossoming as an athlete, my dad exerted great influence over me. He never missed a single game. He never tried to do any coaching when I was in high school, nor did he interfere with the man who was doing the coaching. But he was there when I needed him, and he gave me a lot of good advice about baseball.

Stubborn and troublesome as I was in school and most everywhere else as a kid, I never ever gave my father any lip.

He never once hit me in the face, but he was a strong advocate of corporal punishment. His belief was: If you're punished, you're supposed to hurt. And I did. He'd give me a little rap on the back of the head when I got out of line, and when I really messed things up I got the big, black belt.

I remember one incident during the summer after I had turned twelve. We were playing ball every evening, naturally, but dad's rule was that I was to be home by dark. We had an extra-inning game, a kid named Billy Smith and I fooled around talking with some girls, missed a bus, and it was dark when we got to our neighborhood. I knew I was in a heap of trouble and there was no way I wanted to go into my house. Billy was afraid to leave me, so we found a house under construction and we sat there for hours.

It was just a few doors from our house, and there was a lot of activity around our place. Cars were coming and going. People were yelling. Lights were on. Finally some police cars arrived. Now both of us were frightened out of our wits.

It got to be one thirty or two o'clock in the morning and we knew we couldn't keep our eyes open another minute, so we boldly marched out of that house, Billy down the street to his house and me to mine.

My dad came home a few minutes later and he was saying, "I can't find him. The police can't find him. No one can find him."

Just then he spotted me, standing by my mother.

"This better be good, son. Where have you been?"

I told him what happened, and that I simply was afraid to come home. "I thought you'd kill me."

"I wouldn't have killed you, Dennis, but I am tempted to kill you now."

He did not kill me, of course, but the fact that my rear end didn't fall off completely after the whipping he gave me is testi-

0

mony to my remarkable recuperative powers even at that tender age.

I don't know whether it was before, during, or after the belt treatment that my folks explained why there were police cars all over the place and why everyone was unusually concerned for our safety. Just a week or so before in Chicago, three little brothers were brutally assaulted and murdered. At one stage during the spanking, I might have traded places with them.

Don't get the idea I feared my father. It was nothing like that. I respected his authority and knew enough not to question him. He was working a couple of jobs all the time—he was an insurance adjuster and for a time a truck driver, and I recall him also working in a plant—and he took care of his family.

He saw to it that I got organ lessons when he couldn't really afford them. He played the organ, too.

My dad was no gambler. He might have bet a dollar here and there and I remember the night Rocky Marciano beat Joe Louis the first time, dad was the only one at the Firemen's Club who bet on Marciano and he won the fight pool.

He was a nonviolent guy so far as I know, except on one occasion. He had a whole bunch of kids in the car and we were going down Sunset Avenue. My dad was a guy who drove slowly, especially in a residential area. Just as he turned a corner some guy yelled out, "Slow down, you god-damned son of a bitch."

My dad stopped the car, got out, and approached the guy who was doing all the yelling. Here we were, doing about fifteen miles an hour, and my dad couldn't believe the guy was giving him hell for it.

"Yeah, I'm talking to you, you bastard."

With that, he spit in my dad's face.

My dad gave him a shot right on the kisser and the guy went down in a heap, out cold. The guy wound up in the hospital and my dad wound up paying the hospital bill. But once he whacked the guy, he never said another word, just got back into the car and drove quietly off.

Maybe little incidents like that helped convince me about his authority.

I've always had the premonition that I'd die young.

My dad died when he was thirty-six, two days after his birthday. His father died when he was thirty-five, and his father's father died when he was thirty-five. My father and my

0

great-grandfather died of heart attacks. My grandfather fell out of a tree and a branch pierced his heart.

All three of them were the first-born in their families. And I'm the first-born in ours.

Besides, both my mother's parents died when they were very young.

For a long time, this business of dying young was an obsession with me, and maybe I lived every day as if it would be my last because of this feeling down deep inside me that like those before me in my family, I, too, would die at a very young age.

One more thing—all three of those victims were named Tom. Maybe my being christened Dennis Dale will break the string, I don't know.

My father died May 4, 1959, when I was fifteen.

I had a baseball game on Western Avenue on the South Side of Chicago. My dad never missed a game. I hadn't spotted him by the third inning, and by the time the fifth inning rolled around I figured he had been detained at work. I really wasn't worried about it, though.

After the game, he still hadn't showed up, so I had to figure out a way to get home. Always before, he'd give me a ride. This time, though, I got on the IC, took a shower at school, then got on the bus. It was eight thirty by the time I got home. On the way I stopped to talk with a couple of girls.

We lived on a hill in Markham. It was a nice town. Low- to middle-income families. Nice people.

As I walked up the hill to our house, I noticed a lot of cars around our place. There must have been eight or ten of them. I didn't think much about it.

I walked into the house and everyone just looked at me. No one said as much as "hello." I put my books and my baseball bag down and my mother walked to me and said very simply, "Your father is dead."

I don't think I said a word. If I did, I don't remember. Everything became hazy. I remember walking out of the house and seeing a friend of mine, Bob Hornung. I don't know how long I walked around, but when I came back my dad's car was parked in front of the house, and I remember thinking for a minute that it must have been a bad dream, and that he was alive after all. So I raced back into the house.

He had died, slumped over the wheel of his car, right in

0

front of Comiskey Park. He was on his way to see me pitch when the heart attack got him.

The next few days, even weeks, are a blur in my mind.

I can remember sitting around for three days in that funeral parlor in Harvey, Illinois, and having people come up and tell me how sorry they were. I know people were trying to be nice and all that, but nothing helps at a time like that. No words help. No people help. Nothing helps.

My dad's cousin, a Catholic priest named Father Titus McLain, tried to console me. He was trying to convince me that death should be a time for celebration, not sorrow. I wasn't buying any of that. All I knew was that I loved my dad, and he was gone.

The family had a big gathering at the home of Aunt Delphine Benner. My mother was totally disoriented. She was in a state of shock and unable to make any decisions about anything. Timmy may not have understood what was going on, and I certainly was too young to see any cause for rejoicing at death, no matter how much I thought of the Catholic Church and its teachings.

Right after that, I became very hard. A very cold and unfeeling individual. I quit going to the school functions. I didn't even show up at my senior prom. All I wanted to do was get out of school, then play baseball. Nothing else mattered. It was nothing more than a waiting game, my final two years of high school. I don't know whether I wanted to prove something to myself, or for my father, or what. And I'm not smart enough to figure it out to this day. I don't think he tried to live his life again through me, and I don't think I tried to become the athlete he might have become.

All I know is that when he died, I quit giving a shit about everything except baseball.

I especially didn't give a shit about the man my mother married seven or eight months later.

His name was Tom Clark. He worked with my mother. It was all on the up and up. He was a nice guy and he treated her very well. I guess she figured she needed somebody, and that Timmy and I needed somebody.

Like hell I did.

He was good to her, and he tried to be good to us.

But I wouldn't let him. I hated him, and I let the world know it.

0

She had called Timmy and me together and asked us if we had any objection to her marrying Tom.

Now, what the hell am I gonna say? I'm fifteen, she obviously needs someone, he obviously cares a great deal for her, so how the hell do I rear up and say, "Yes, mother, as a matter of fact, I'm not too pleased about the current state of affairs and it would be my hope that you would reconsider"?

Naturally, Timmy and I told her it was fine with us.

I gritted my teeth when I said it.

In my mind, anyway, my father was too soon gone, and here was another guy with my mother, sleeping in my father's bed and playing the father role with two boys. I couldn't stand any of it. I resented him, and I resented my mother for caring for him.

Tom was generous and hardworking. He was always giving me money; maybe to get rid of me, who knows? But he taught me to drive, helped me get my driver's license, and did everything in the world for us.

As I look back on it, Tom was just a super human being. He wasn't trying to take my father's place, but rather just trying to assist us where my father couldn't. I was very wrong, and I was very selfish.

There's no question in anyone's mind that I broke up their marriage. The divorce papers were filed while I was still in high school. They stayed married only a couple of years, because I put the blocks to their relationship.

Today, Timmy and I are just starting to communicate again. We were close in the glory days and he worked for me in Atlanta when I owned a club; then we had a falling out over money and I sent him packing.

Naturally, my mother took Timmy's part. She's always favored him. He's younger, has less ability, had fewer breaks, and much of the time along the line he's worked for me. And that's not a healthy situation.

He's more Irish than Polish. Timmy doesn't care much about anything or anybody, even himself. He'll help people, if he can, but he lives a day at a time and sometimes gives the impression he's not too concerned about whether he wakes up the next morning.

Maybe Timmy and I will get back together and have a close relationship, I don't know. But it's never been like a brotherly relationship should be.

0

As for my mother and I, we just are not friendly toward each other.

She wasn't even invited to our wedding reception. Sharyn and I eloped, but had a reception later in Chicago. Some of my aunts and uncles were there, but we were afraid mom would make a big scene. She was totally opposed to my getting married. Figured we were too young and that it wouldn't work out.

"You're not mature enough," she'd say. "Kids can't make it the way things are priced today."

I told her she and dad made it, but her answer was always the same, "Times are different now."

It made no sense to me. I was in love with Sharyn then and I'm in love with Sharyn today, despite all the trouble I've caused her.

I'm certain my mother didn't resent Sharyn or dislike her as a person—she would have resented anyone coming into my life then.

We've never really sat down and discussed these things. I know things should be different now. I know they should have been different all along. We simply never communicated about our problems, so they just grew.

In 1968 we got together for a while. It was more of a truce than a reconciliation and all the family was together because of the pennant and the World Series.

My mother is great with my children. She sees them regularly and is generous with them and I'm sure she loves them to pieces. In the fall of 1974 Sharyn and I were driving in Chicago with the four kids and we weren't too far from my mom's house. She'd been mad at me ever since I fired Timmy in 1972, and we hadn't spoken for more than a year.

But I said to Sharyn, "I think we ought to go see my mother."

When we went through that door, my mother broke down. It was a moment to remember. I just couldn't believe it. She was so happy. Still, we didn't talk about the things that had kept us apart, and perhaps we never will.

She's married now, and has been for six or seven years to a wonderful guy named Jack Lecki. Even when she married him, I had my mind made up that I wouldn't like him. But they've been great for each other.

It took me a long time to realize that life goes on when there is death or divorce or whatever. People have a right to

0

live, and while they are living, a right to try to get as much happiness and contentment out of life as they can.

As a father, I've tried to pattern myself after my own father. No matter how long I've been away, when I come home the four kids are all over me, and we romp and play. But when I get serious with them, they know it, and they mind.

Now, my kids aren't perfect by any stretch of the imagination. They're active and ornery and lovable and coy and conniving—I guess like all children.

We adopted our two sons, but believe me they're as much our children, in every way, as the two girls. And I can say in all candor that the only difference is that I didn't sire them and they didn't come out of Sharyn's womb. But they're ours, heart and soul and mind and body.

Kristin, our older daughter, is typical McLain, and in some ways that's exasperating. Ask her why she did something and she's apt to say, "Because I wanted to, that's why."

But when you speak firmly, she totally comprehends and she gets her act together.

Our little one, Michelle, is a wall-banger. Sharyn and I have kidded that God sent us Michelle to punish us for our wrongdoings—past, present, and future. She's our "Eloise."

Sharyn got a bowl of goldfish for the kids. I guess there were seven fish originally. I say originally because Michelle and the cat obviously did a number on them. It must have been one great race to see who'd get at the goldfish first, Michelle or the cat.

We kept the bowl on Krissie's dresser, knowing the three older kids wouldn't bother the fish and assuming a tot of two and a half couldn't lug the thing around.

Wrong again!

We thought she was upstairs taking her afternoon nap when Sharyn hears this splashing sound and some chattering and meowing. Michelle had carried the fishbowl into our bedroom and, one by one, picked them out of the bowl and put them on the bed. They're flopping around, gasping and jerking all over the place, and Michelle is trying to smack them, apparent to keep things quiet. Meanwhile the cat is sitting on the edge of the bed looking very full.

Of the seven original fish, four survived the ordeal, two were pronounced dead on arrival and one is still missing in action. The consensus is that he found a warm home in the cat's stomach.

O

The immediate problem was to replace the missing fish so Kris wouldn't notice when she came home from school. So Sharyn rushed out and bought three of those little fake goldfish—the inflatable kind—and dropped them into the tank. Kris never noticed, and a week or so later Sharyn was able to remove the artificial fish without upsetting Kris because she's only interested in anything for about a week or so.

Kris is a little lady and probably will wind up being homecoming queen and breaking some young man's heart.

Michelle will break some guy's leg.

Kris has a new boyfriend every day and I get the news about the newest flame each day after school. At age nine, she has discovered boys and she likes what she sees.

While Kris is reigning as queen, Michelle will be a star in the roller derby or a demolition derby.

Dennis is very studious and loves to draw. He'll probably wind up flying to Mars because he loves anything that moves, and the faster the better. I've had him with me countless times in a plane, and he never wants to land. He just loves it up there and is totally content when he's in the air.

Timmy is extremely well-coordinated. He's a left-hander and does everything well. His whole life is sports and he doesn't have much time for anything else. When time comes for dinner, he's too worn out from playing to care much about food.

I've been asked if my on-again, off-again relationship with Sharyn has hurt the kids. I don't think so. Their whole life has been spent moving from one place to another and they're accustomed to it. They've learned to roll with the punches, and, in all, I don't think the background of a baseball family is all that bad if you use common sense. Kids who have had to make some adjustments early in life, I think, are a lot better suited to take the knocks they're bound to get later on.

My kids are very much in awe of God, even the word "God." Sharyn and I have taught them to respect God and to believe that He's everywhere.

I'm an old Catholic in a lot of ways: I prefer the mass in Latin, I think we should not eat meat on Fridays, I think confession is good for the soul, and I'm not much for Saturday evening masses or those rock masses.

On the other hand, I believe a person can have a good, working relationship with God regardless of his or her faith,

0

and I wouldn't run out and slash my wrists if one of my children decided to marry someone of another faith.

I guess what I'm trying to say is that I believe certain things, and not even all Catholics agree with me. If you believe something else, that's fine with me. If it works for you, that's beautiful. As for me, I'm not the person I should be, and I never have been, and it bothers me.

Baseball is a game designed to be fun. The fact that so-called grown men play it for huge sums of money shouldn't mean that it ceases to be fun. I doubt seriously if Abner Doubleday envisioned player strikes, disputes between players and owners, and all that. He probably didn't even think that someday two teams would trade managers, as the Tigers and Indians once did with Jimmy Dykes and Joe Gordon.

I always had fun with baseball, even if at times I had to go out and create it myself. And the players I could never tolerate were the ones so single-minded that baseball was the only thing on their minds. I know I've always been a good competitor. But that doesn't mean it can't be fun there, too. The greatest thrill I could ever experience is the personal duel between a pitcher and a batter. It's the game within the game.

As a kid growing up I lived and breathed baseball. It was a way of life for me and for the kids in my neighborhood. I'm not convinced that it builds character or anything else. I think it's a lot like any other endeavor. A man is what he is, and what he is is a result of his heredity and environment, the type of family he has, the type of friends, his schooling, the brains God gave him to start with, and the type of atmosphere in which he lived.

Only Ted Williams succeeded in keeping me from having fun, but still I managed to sneak away and have a laugh once in a while—a couple of times at his expense.

Many times the fun backfired, and quite often people didn't understand.

There was a great deal of misunderstanding about the home run pitch I threw to Mickey Mantle after we had clinched the pennant in 1968. All the pressure was gone. I had won my thirtieth the previous Saturday. It was funsville the rest of the way, and here we were facing the Yankees in a meaningless game for everyone. Sure, I wanted to win, and I never would have deliberately grooved a pitch to Mick had it meant anything.

But I had a 6–1 lead, and there wasn't a soul on base. And let's be honest, Mantle was going after one of those home run milestones and he's always been one of my very favorite people.

The first pitch I tossed up there to him had no velocity on it at all. Matter of fact, it was a sort of humpbacked thing. Mantle couldn't believe his eyes. The iron mike machine pitches better than that.

0

Bill Freehan was catching and he couldn't call time fast enough. He came out to the mound in that "Big Ten trot" and asked me, "What in the hell is going on?"

Now, isn't that ridiculous? I'm a kid from Chicago's South Side. He's a guy with a college education, and I have to tell him what's happening.

"Just tell Mantle to be ready. The next one will be right down the cock as soft as I can get it up there."

I just wanted to see how far Mickey could hit one. In my time I've had some of those rockets hit off me and I thought Mickey might as well drive one into Canada for this historic home run if he could do it. I certainly wasn't going to do anything to keep him from getting the record.

The next pitch was a silly little thing that arced over the plate, and again, Mickey just stood there. Apparently Freehan and Mantle had a communications problem. Mickey had asked Bill, "What the hell's he doing out there?"

Bill apparently told Mantle he wasn't at all sure.

Now, Freehan is out to the mound again. I had given Mantle two pitches right down the middle. He never budged. Hell, people in the stands knew what was going on. Why was it so difficult for Mantle and Freehan to figure it out?

I had thrown him two loop-de-loops with nothing on them but the seams. I'll admit I was tempted to hum one right past him because I really had him set up for it. But I actually wanted the Mick to blast one. Finally the message got through to him, and he broke into a grin. Then he gave *me* a signal, with his right hand, showing me where he wanted the next one, right out over the plate, waist high.

In those days my control was pretty good, and that's where I put the next one, with about as much speed on it as your average eight-year-old can muster. Mantle hit it a mile. Someone said the baseball hit a seat in the upper deck so hard it broke one of the boards.

Mickey wasn't one to jump up and down as he made the trip around the bases, because he'd made that route only four million times before. But as he crossed home plate and headed for the Yankee dugout, he turned and bowed to me and yelled out, "Thanks."

I was laughing my belly button off. It didn't matter to me how hard he hit it. I was just glad to do it for him.

Next man up for New York is Joe Pepitone. He thought he'd get the same treatment. At least he asked for it.

0

"Fast ball!" he ordered as he got ready to step into the batter's box.

I shook my head no.

"Curve ball?"

He was looking for any help he could get.

"Change-up?"

"Slider?"

"God damn you, McLain, tell me something."

So I took my finger and motioned to the side of my head, then I threw a fast ball up and in, toward his head. Joe hit the dust. At the time, I thought it was funnier than hell. Joe understood my humor, apparently. He didn't get hot.

I knew when that game started if the opportunity came up, I'd let Mantle hit the home run that put him third on the all-time home run list. There never was any question about it, although I didn't announce it on the public address system.

It turns out later when Freehan and Mantle were chatting, the message Freehan relayed to Mantle was, "Denny says for you to be ready."

And Mantle wondered, "What the hell does that mean?"

Ready to hit, or ready to hit the dirt?

Mantle got his home run, Pepitone got struck out, and I got in more trouble. The manager, Mayo Smith, heard from the office of the commissioner. Something about the integrity of the great game of baseball being at stake and all that bullshit. I ignored it, and until now I've never admitted that I deliberately grooved one to my friend Mickey.

I used to talk to the hitters all the time.

I remember pitching against Kansas City one time and Joe Foy was in one terrible slump. He was something like zero for forty-six and we had a big lead with Joe at the plate.

"Fast ball, Joe," I yelled and the idiot took it for a strike.

"Slider coming this time, Joe."

Damned if he didn't take it for strike two. I was beginning to think I'd have to tee it up for him.

The two of us only had one more chance. By this time Joe is beginning to believe me and he looked out for some encouraging word. He got it. "Sidearm fast ball."

I threw a pretty good one, too, down and away, but Joe hit that thing nine miles. All I could see going around the bases was those white teeth.

Later that night Joe and I met in a bar for a drink.

O

"Man, you're crazy," he said. "How can one motherfucker be that goofy?"

"Look at it this way, Joe. You're oh for forty-six. If you don't get a hit sometime, they're gonna send you down. And I don't want you in the minor leagues. You can't help me there, Joe. I can stand you on your head any time I want to, and I need all the Joe Foys I can get."

We had another laugh, and probably another drink.

One time in Birmingham I found out they had a deal with jackpot money for a home run in a certain inning. The guy who hits it splits the jackpot with some fan in the stands. We were down by a hundred runs or so and it was late in the ball game and I let some kid hit one out.

The ungrateful little shithead never even thanked me.

That's the difference in a major leaguer and a bush leaguer. Mantle had class.

I've met all kinds in baseball. You name the type, I've played with them. Introverts. Extroverts. Exhibitionists. Con men. Alcoholics and pill-poppers. I've played with the most selfish athletes in the world, and the greatest team men the game has ever known. I said it before, but baseball has the same kind of people in it that any other business has. There are some guys who'd qualify for man-of-the-year awards and guys who should be kept in cages.

The flakiest player I ever encountered was a pitcher named Bill Faul.

He was briefly with the Tigers and had all the physical equipment to make it. But he kept his head up his ass most of the time and the resultant oxygen shortage must have affected him.

Bill was a great advocate of hypnosis. Matter of fact, I've always felt Bill was in a trance all the time.

He was a short, stocky guy and very strong, in top physical shape. He threw almost everything 95 percent sidearm. He had a good, live fast ball and a brain that had passed away.

I first met Faul when I joined the Tigers and was sent to their minor league headquarters at Tigertown in Lakeland, Florida. We all stayed in those army barracks, and Faul was one of the main attractions in an otherwise dull camp.

He boasted he could hypnotize anyone. Naturally, the day came when he insisted on trying to put me under. I figured

0

"what the hell," and so I let him begin. A bunch of the guys were standing around kibitzing, some of them believing, I suppose, and others throwing out insults. Nothing deterred Bill Faul. He had me sit in a chair. He extracted an old pocket watch from his slacks.

"You will follow my every move. You will follow the watch. Back and forth. Back and forth. Concentrate on the watch. Watch the watch very closely. Do not take your eyes off this watch. Think of nothing else, and listen to what I tell you. You will see only the watch and you will hear only my voice, no matter what these assholes are saying."

Soon I closed my eyes. He ordered me to stand. I stood. He told me to walk around the room and down the hallway. I did exactly as he ordered.

We came upon a little table.

"Climb up on the table, Denny," he said.

I climbed atop the table.

"Now, you will walk off the table onto the floor without hurting yourself."

"Fuck you, Faul. The game is over."

Everyone broke up, but Faul didn't think it was funny.

He and I were on the same team in winter ball in Puerto Rico and Bob Swift was the manager. Faul had been bombed out in the fifth or sixth inning and he was plenty pissed when Swift took him out.

Joe Sparma and I were playing gin rummy when Faul stormed into the locker room. We thought he was going to climb the walls. He was throwing things all over the place and was mad as hell at Swift for taking him out.

"Shit, there's no way I should have come out of there. I had good stuff. God damn him, anyway. I wanted to stay in that ball game."

He was always pretty well excited by nature, but this night he was superhyper. I honestly thought he was going to ruin the locker room.

Mad as he was, I got him to sit down and listen to me.

"If you want to pitch so much, why don't you go back out there and pitch. Just put on someone else's uniform and go out there and start pitching again."

Maybe he really was in a trance, but he was taking all of it in, and Sparma wasn't hurting our cause.

"Hell yes, Bill," said Joe. "If I felt the way you do, I'd put on somebody else's shirt and march my ass back out there."

O

Faul wasn't laughing, so we knew he was buying. Good old Sparma. He cemented the deal. Joe raced over and grabbed another uniform. Before Faul could back out of the deal, we were helping him on with the shirt.

When our team came in to hit, we grabbed the pitcher—I can't remember who it was. We made it clear to him he wasn't going back out there. When our guys went into the field again, Faul went right with them. Matter of fact, the crazy bastard ran to the mound and started warming up.

The catcher didn't say anything and Swift didn't even notice it until the umpire started screaming.

"You're out of the game already."

"Up your ass," said Faul. "I've got another number so that makes me legal again."

Suddenly it dawns on Bob Swift what's happening and he's out to that mound like a shot and he fines Faul two hundred bucks. When he got back to the dugout, Sparma and I are splitting a gut laughing and it was no secret who had cooked up the deal.

Swift then announced Faul wouldn't be fined, and that instead Sparma and I would be fined a hundred bucks each.

We were together later in Syracuse. Faul had a thing about taking showers. I mean, he didn't like them. He must not have liked them. He didn't take them very often. I mean, he didn't always take them even *after* he pitched.

One night after a game he pitched Faul complained of a sore back and got into the whirlpool. He put his head back and closed his eyes and for all we knew his mind was in South America. We sneaked in with a big box of detergent and slowly dumped the whole thing into the whirlpool. Suddenly the shower room became one giant bubble bath and Faul jumped out cussing and snorting.

"I'll kill the sonofabitch who did this."

Until now, Mr. Faul hasn't had a clue.

John Wyatt was a pitcher who spent some time in the major leagues, principally because he had one of the game's all-time great spitters. I've heard of guys using spit, some kind of bark they chew, vaseline, you name it—but John Wyatt used that hemorrhoid solution stuff called Preparation H.

Don't ask me where he kept it!

John, who later pitched for the Tigers briefly, was pitching against us one night for the Boston Red Sox and his catcher,

O

Jose Azcue, threw a shot right through the mound to try to get a runner trying to steal second base. The ball had to be going seventy-five miles an hour and it hit Wyatt right in the head and knocked him down and the damned ball bounced almost into the stands. I mean it was a direct hit.

Wyatt calmly picked himself up and struck out the batter. Now, that's using your head.

Another time when he was pitching for us in '68 Emmet Ashford, the majors' first black umpire, was working behind the plate. Wyatt's spitter was dropping a foot and a half that night and finally the batters were bitching so much that Emmet just had to make a trip to the mound. He told John he knew he was doctoring up the baseball and that it simply had to quit.

"Emmet," said John, "I've been throwin' this here pitch a long, long time and it's keepin' me alive. But this is the first time I just cain't help being illegal. You know something, Emmet, I got the worst case of piles you ever saw, and I got that Preparation H crap all over my body and some of it bound to get on that baseball tonight."

And he did, indeed, have it everywhere: under his arms, in his glove, you name it. If someone had struck a match around Wyatt that night it would have looked like a Ku Klux Klan rally.

It's been said a thousand times before, but sometimes you win baseball games that you have no business winning. You have absolutely nothing on the ball, and still the hitters can't touch you. Other times, with super stuff, you get the crap knocked out of you.

I never was much good in spring training. My arm hurt, my shoulder was tight and it took me a long time to get into pitching shape. After a while, I didn't worry so much about getting knocked around because I knew what I could do, and the whole purpose of training camp was to get ready for the season.

When I got to the Oakland Athletics, Manager Dick Williams had some difficulty understanding that. My first time out in spring training for the Athletics I got bounced around for eighty or ninety hits in six innings. All I saw of the outfield was elbows and assholes.

After the game, Williams came up to me in the clubhouse and inquired about my health.

"I'm fine. Don't worry. This happens every spring."

Two or three days later, I'm due to pitch again and Williams

0

yelled out to the outfielders, "You guys don't have to do your running and wind sprints today. McLain's pitching. You'll get plenty of running during the normal course of events."

A very funny man, Dick Williams.

I'll bet he's not nearly that funny now that he's managing the Angels.

One time when baseball was no fun at all—when I was enduring my year under Theodore Williams—I had a fast ball that wasn't moving, a curve ball that was hanging, and a slider I couldn't get over the plate. Yet I shut out the Angels 4–0.

A good friend of mine, Jim Fregosi, got a hanging curve ball right in the meat of the plate and popped it up to second base. It was a pitch he should have hit into the Pacific Ocean. When Jim came back across the mound he said, "Where'd you get that shit you're throwing tonight. I don't see how you get anybody out with that."

It was good-natured fun, and Jimmy couldn't believe he didn't hit that garbage either.

Moments like that helped make for a little fun in an otherwise drab season.

I never had a no-hitter in the major leagues. I flirted with one several times.

The best game I ever pitched was in 1965 or 1966, I don't exactly remember when. But it was against Cleveland and Sonny Siebert was pitching for the Indians and has us beat 1–0 for seven innings until Don Demeter hit a two-run homer and won it for us. I made about 110 pitches that night and only one of them was bad. It was a fast ball, cock high, and someone hit it into the upper deck. I gave up another hit or two, I guess, but I'll always remember that night because it was the first time I pitched the ball where I wanted it to go.

There wasn't a single walk in nine innings and I struck out a dozen. Dressen was managing then. After the game he was telling the press, "I told you so. Didn't I tell you the kid was gonna be a big league pitcher?"

Charlie knew I was an ornery cuss, but didn't give me much hell about it. Mayo Smith knew it, too, and for a time attempted to "handle" me, as he put it. It became a losing battle, but I often was blamed for things I had nothing to do with.

Once, when we were staying at the Grand Hotel in Anaheim, they had an old vintage airplane out on the lawn of the hotel. We had thrown a party because we knew we were going to win the pennant, and the party got very drunk and went on until three in the morning. I wasn't much of a drinker then— and I'm still not very good at it—so I hit the sack at about 1:30 A.M.

My phone rang at 4:00 A.M. and someone said, "Denny, you and your buddies who put that airplane in the pool get out there right now and get it out of the pool." And he hung up.

I didn't put any airplane in any pool and to this day don't know who did it. But I got some of the guys—Sparma, Aguirre, and someone else—and we went out there and somehow yanked this airplane out of the water.

Baseball players are a lot like little children some of the time. I'm sure this will come as a great shock to Little Leaguers everywhere, but there are times when major league athletes show no more maturity than their tiny counterparts.

Once, on a never-ending trip to Seattle, one of the Detroit Tiger players "appropriated" the megaphone, or bullhorn, stewardesses use to broadcast messages on board the plane. To this day, I don't know who took it, but naturally Mayo Smith blamed me for it.

Frankly, I was very seriously involved in a pinochle game that began before takeoff and was totally innocent. When we landed, the pilot announced a massive land and sea search for the missing megaphone. Then Mayo Smith got on the horn and announced that not a soul would leave the airplane until the damned thing was found. He said he and the coaches would put their heads down, or turn their backs on the players, and that the guilty party should produce the megaphone.

Suddenly, *two* megaphones come flying out of nowhere. Someone had stolen the one in the back of the plane, too.

Kid stuff! But when you're dealing with kids, that's what happens sometimes.

Early in my career with the Tigers we had a pitcher by the name of Ed Rakow. He had a great deal of confidence but no one understood why. One time we were playing a game in Kansas City and Rakow was the starter. He went through the first three innings and they never saw the baseball. He had an extraordinary curve ball and it was breaking a foot and a half that night. After three innings Ed strutted into the dugout and announced, "Boys, pay close attention because tonight you're gonna see history."

He didn't retire another batter the rest of the game.

O

Rakow's performance that night reminded me of the story of the magician who was entertaining dinner guests at the captain's table on the *Titanic* and announced he was about to pull off his best trick. Next thing anyone knew they were splashing around in the ocean trying to keep from drowning and someone spotted the magician holding onto a piece of debris, and asked:

"What are you, some kind of a nut?"

"This is Denny McLain Enterprises, Ray Oyler speaking. Mr. McLain is not available."

That's the way my buddy, Ray Oyler, answered the phone much of the time in 1968. Things were so hectic that we held all the calls until noon. Calls came in from everywhere, all the time. I could have done a lot to discourage some of them, but I love to talk, and I don't ever remember turning down an interview. I might have postponed some because I was so busy, but I tried to be responsive to the needs of the press.

As for the other calls, you just never knew when another deal would be on the fire.

One day, one of the newsmen decided to interview Oyler, to see what it was like to be the roommate of Dennis Dale McLain.

"You caught me on an exceptionally good day," Ray told him, "because today something very exciting happened in my life. The phone in our room rang, and it was for *me.*"

When the story appeared, there was one quote from Ray that made me feel as good as anything in the newspapers ever has.

"All this attention Denny's getting doesn't seem to bother him at all. When he pitches, he gets the job done. He takes it all in stride. All the attention could make him a real smart-aleck, but he hasn't changed a bit from the guy I roomed with four years ago."

We kidded Ray a lot about his hitting, and he took that in stride, too. He hit one home run in all the 1968 season, and when he did it I told him that one home run convinced me the baseball was doctored.

I've talked freely and openly about my gambling. I really have nothing to hide. It's impossible to hide something when the whole world has been informed about it.

0

When I was pitching in Birmingham, after being sent down by the A's, I was approached about throwing a game.

I know this may sound ludicrous, and even to think that there could be that amount of money bet on a minor league baseball game seems farfetched. But I had been playing golf with some guys I met and two guys (they were brothers) in the foursome volunteered to drive me back to the city.

The first time my ears perked up was when one of the brothers said how nice it'd be if a guy just knew, without a doubt, when one team was going to win.

I allowed as how you could bet your house, your car, and your mother-in-law on that.

"Have you ever thought about that sort of thing, Denny?" one of them asked.

At that moment, I knew it was a specific inquiry, not a general one. I told them it had never occurred to me, and I explained something that perhaps even high-rollers don't think about: "A pitcher could try to throw the game, but if he's deliberately horseshit, he's gonna come out of there and another pitcher is gonna be put in. And what if the team that's behind comes roaring from behind. What then?"

They had an answer for that.

"In your position, they don't take you out so quickly. After all, you're Denny McLain. You're trying to work yourself into shape, and you can talk the manager into letting you stay in the game a little longer."

I said nothing.

Then the other brother piped up: "How are you fixed for money?"

I lied and told them I was okay.

"But anyone could always use an extra twenty-five thousand dollars, couldn't he?"

Jesus Christ! How can someone be talking about twenty-five big ones in Birmingham? If he's willing to give me that much, how much is he betting?

They told me just to think about it. I did. Plenty. But think is all I did.

Two days later I was on my way to join the Atlanta Braves, and I've never seen those guys again.

I know it'd make me sound very principled to add right here that I never would have entertained the thought of doing such a thing. All I'll say is that I'm glad I never really had to face the decision. I'd like to think in my own mind that I'd have enough character to resist such a temptation, but I'm not convinced of it—especially if the money came in front, in small, unmarked bills in a plain, manila envelope.

Baseball officials would have the fan believe that gambling is nonexistent in baseball. That's not true. Instead, it's almost a way of life. Many baseball players—and I'm sure it's true in other sports—spend more time in card games than they do at their work.

As I told you, my Tiger teammates once dubbed me The Dolphin because I was such a big fish. Fine and dandy. I can't argue with that. But if I was a dolphin, then Brant Alyea was the great white whale.

One day when I was with the Athletics a bunch of us were sitting around watching the Pro Bowlers Tour on ABC television, and Alyea started popping off about how good a bowler he was. Hell, I had been carrying a 200-plus average in several leagues around Detroit just a couple of seasons before that, so we went from the bullshit to the challenge. I told Alyea I wouldn't pick up a sixteen-pound bowling ball for any bet less than $100 a game and $200 a series.

By the end of the evening, I owned him. It went from that to golf, and I owned him there.

Ken Holtzman was my partner and Rollie Fingers teamed up with Alyea.

As I owned Alyea, Holtzman owned Fingers.

Brant wound up owing me $16,000 for golf and bowling. I got an occasional hundred bucks or so, and that's all. I even went to Charlie Finley to try to get my money, but he didn't want to get involved.

Fingers owed Holtzman $4,000 and Holtzman used to reduce the debt by having Rollie serve as his gopher.

"Get me a Coke."

"Get it yourself."

"Get me a Coke and I'll knock fifty bucks off what you owe me."

Fingers got the Coke for Kenny.

I had become pretty good at card games by the time I left Detroit, and won lots of money playing against my teammates with the Washington Senators. The other guys called my winnings the McLain Contribution Fund.

We started a hearts game after a Saturday night game and I

0

was up a couple hundred dollars and we had been playing for two or three hours. I was dead tired and announced I was quitting after the next round of deals.

"No way you're quitting," said Dick Billings. "You're too far ahead. You have to give us a chance to get even."

Next thing I knew there was a hissing sound underneath the card table. Billings had taken a can of hair spray and turned it on full steam and put a match to it. Coming out from under that table was the damndest blue flame you ever saw and as I looked down, I swallowed what seemed to be a foot of that blue torch.

I was gagging and rolling around on the floor, convinced I'd never speak again. Not pitching again is bad enough, but Denny McLain not being able to talk? Ridiculous! For a couple of hours, I was in considerable discomfort—but within minutes I knew life would go on. And so did the card game, for three more hours.

I still won, though.

Some baseball players never fool around on their wives. Others do it once in a while. Still others consider a road trip a total disaster if they didn't get lucky, even if the team won every game.

But every player who fools around much gets caught. It's inevitable. There's just no way to avoid it. Baseball players must be the dumbest lot of people in the world when it comes to covering up their extra-marital tracks. Maybe they want to get caught. One of those educated psychologists once said that every man who cheats really wants—down deep inside—to get caught. I can't speak for all players, but I never ever harbored any desire, secret or otherwise, to get caught. I went to great lengths to avoid it—then wound up, as all cheaters do—making some idiotic move that opened the floodgates.

There are standard lines for everything, and I'm not making any startling revelations that players and players' wives haven't heard, and most likely discussed before.

You have lipstick on your collar and the line is that you must have brushed up against a stewardess or a fan. You know how fans press up against their pet players.

A gushy letter left carelessly in your pocket, or an errant telephone number and the line is that it's from some screwball broad who writes to a ton of players, or the phone number is

0

that of a fan who wants you to send her an autographed picture.

Players who get caught generally get caught because they carry phone numbers around with them—and because they have suspicious wives who check those things. One of my teammates once packed in a hurry on the last day of a road trip, and quite by accident stuffed in his suitcase the blouse of a woman who had spent the night nursing him back to health.

His wife helped him unpack and they both noticed the blouse at the same time. Like most athletes, he had great reactions and he quickly gave it to his wife as a present. What a thoughtful husband! Here he is on the road, away from wife and kiddies, battling a prolonged batting slump, and yet he takes the time to go shopping and return home bearing a gift.

The blouse was size thirty-two.

His wife of eleven years wore size thirty-eight.

No sale.

THE GAME

11

WITHIN THE GAME

In many ways, baseball is a ridiculous game. A good pitcher is off work three out of every four days. A batter can flunk out seven times out of ten and still become a candidate for Cooperstown. And at the very worst, you're working only eight months out of the year.

And amazingly enough, lots of people with precious little ability make it to the big leagues—not just as players, but as coaches, managers, front office people, and umpires. And I almost forgot, as commissioners, too.

It isn't an original line with me, but someone said Ford Frick proved that baseball could do without a commissioner. The late General William Eckert was commissioner and he didn't know whether the ball was round or whether it had seams or laces.

The guy who has the job now is trying to be a tough guy commissioner like Judge Landis and if he's not careful the owners will boot him out on his hind end. Bowie Kuhn realizes he is a tool of the owners, as all commissioners for years have been, and it's obvious he's beginning to feel some of the strength of the office and likes the feel of that muscle.

He flexed those muscles pretty good in suspending me—and even then got criticized because some people said my punishment wasn't severe enough. What did they want, a public hanging?

He's warned Charlie Finley a couple of times, but I honestly think the commissioner is a little afraid of Charlie because Kuhn knows that old rascal might make life pretty miserable for him.

More recently, Kuhn sat Yankee owner George Steinbrenner III down for a couple of years for those illegal campaign contributions to former President Nixon's 1972 drive for reelection.

I noticed the other owners in baseball didn't rally around and applaud Kuhn for that move! That's getting pretty close to home, slapping one of his owners. And the owners are the ones who hire and fire commissioners. After the owners got rid of Happy Chandler, they established a pattern of never hiring a strong commissioner.

The title's all wrong anyway. Kuhn shouldn't be called the commissioner of baseball. He should be called the commissioner for the owners. He's in no position to be fair and impartial and objective. How can he be, when he's the owners' man and not the players'?

0

But his powers are there, and they have been all along. They're spelled right out in Article I—it's incumbent upon the commissioner to investigate either on complaint or his own initiative any acts suspected of not being in the best interests of baseball; and section B of that same article gives him the authority to determine any punitive action.

And every player who signs a major league contract has it spelled out for him—the dangers and possible penalties for actions contrary to the best interests of baseball.

This doesn't help the poor slob who slipped through high school without learning the meaning of words like "incumbent" and "punitive," or the guy who simply doesn't bother reading his contract. I read mine a whole lot closer after I got into trouble.

Bitter? Sure, I'm bitter. But it's not a bitterness that I can't live with, because for a time I had it, I did it, and no one can take all that away from me.

And while I had it, despite all the difficulties, I loved it. As much as I wanted to play shortstop as a kid, I fell in love just with the idea of being a pitcher.

Someone who pitches gets more personal satisfaction out of the game than anyone else. I know a catcher is the only player who can see all eight other players right in the chops and you can call him the quarterback of the baseball team if you like—but the game basically is in the hands of the pitcher.

To my way of thinking, the absolute epitome of a major league pitching performance is for a starting pitcher to work every fourth day, pitch 250 innings a year, and go 9 innings almost every time out. The finest accomplishment a pitcher can have is a shutout and I went for that every time out. Once the shutout was ruined, I tended to relax a little if my team had a reasonable lead.

My strategy always was to go out and throw hell out of the ball and figure my team would score a few runs for me. Fortunately, most of the teams I played with did just that—especially the Detroit Tigers of 1968. I always had trouble in the early going because I had trouble getting loose, perhaps because of my muscle structure. I knew if I got by the first couple of innings, things would be okay, and my teammates knew that, too.

When I'd lose a shutout, it took a certain amount of fun out of the game. There was a great feeling of power, knowing that I

0

had control over a situation. It was actually a kick watching batters' futility. I enjoyed being the master over "them."

And I never screwed around with any pitch when I had a shutout going.

Do you suppose that's an unkind streak in me? I imagine someone will psychoanalyze it that way.

I don't know how much of baseball or pitching is psychology, but the percentage is pretty high. I'm sure that in 1968 and 1969 I had lots of teams pretty well defeated when we took the field. I was going hot, they knew it, and I knew it. That gave us a pretty good edge going in.

The late Vince Lombardi said he figured football was 75 percent psychology. Pitching has to be almost that much, too.

There is nothing quite so stimulating, nothing quite so dramatic, as the game within the game—that one-to-one duel between pitcher and batter.

It's the only thing I really miss about baseball, and I swear that's true.

I got so excited about that part of the game I almost peed my pants. It's a very personal thing, one man's ability against that of another man. There is no gray area to any of it—it's plain black and plain white. Either you do it or he does it to you.

The confrontation is the thing!

The game was fun for me but that isn't to say I didn't take it seriously. It's just that I never forgot how to laugh when it got funny.

I probably talked more to batters than any pitcher in the history of the game.

When I first came to the big leagues, Ted Uhlaender of the Twins used to hit me real well. Then I started talking to him and I think I fucked up his concentration. I used to tell him what I was going to throw to him, and he went crazy at the plate.

Here's a guy who used to hit nothing but line drives against me when he was guessing with me. But when I started saying, "Teddy, next one's a high curve ball," he'd pop it up. When I needed a double play, I'd tell him he was getting a low curve ball, I'd throw it, and damned if he didn't chop it into the ground for two.

I used to talk to Kenny Harrelson all the time and he couldn't buy a hit off me. And I'd yell at Joe Pepitone and always ask him where he was going after the game. I'd get him thinking about anything other than baseball, then I owned him.

I'd talk to big George Scott, too, and he'd talk back to me. In general, I had pretty good success against him.

I talked to Roy White of the Yankees a lot, too, but I couldn't get to him. The more I talked, the harder he hit the ball. Roy had great concentration.

Gene Michael was another guy I couldn't reach. Here's a fellow who probably hasn't hit more than ten home runs in his life and he's hit half of them against me. If you teed the ball up for Michael, he'd bat no more than .250, but he must have hit .500 against me, and I'll never figure out the reason. You can choose to call me a liar if you like, but later in my career I actually pitched around Gene Michael because he owned my ass.

One of the last games I pitched for Oakland was against the Yankees and Michael beat me with a home run after I had two strikes on him. And I made some good pitches against him, and even when I'd put the ball right where I wanted to, he'd chink it up the middle or bloop it into short center for a hit.

I talked to two of the strongest men in baseball, Frank Howard and Harmon Killebrew. Both are class guys and fine hitters, but I had uncommon success against them. A typical conversation with Howard was:

"Okay, you big shithead, I'm gonna pitch you inside, right to your strength. Just make sure you pull the ball, dummy."

I always thanked God for Don Wert at third base. He handled more chances from Frank Howard than any other batter in the history of the game.

I always wanted to kid around with Mickey Mantle, but I was too much in awe of him to screw around much. He'd been my hero too long, so I never said much more than hello.

Reggie Jackson hit two big home runs off me the day I won my thirtieth, but outside of that he never got much off me. I used to love to challenge him with that great big swing of his, then send his ass back to the bench talking to himself.

The Punch-and-Judy hitters gave me more trouble than the big swingers. Dick Green used to make a living off me. Matter of fact, he'd talk to me and beg me to throw him a hanging curve ball. And more than once in a while, I did, and he'd rap out another base hit off me.

The one man who absolutely owned my butt was Boog Powell. I'd have paid off his pension to get him to retire. If

O

Boog could have hit against me every day of his life, he'd have been put into the Hall of Fame by voice vote.

And I tried everything, believe me. I'd talk with him before a game but he'd just grin. Once in a while, I'd say something to make him laugh and I'd think, "Hell, I got him now because his concentration is broken."

Boog never needed concentration to hit whatever I threw up there. All he needed was a bat in his hands.

Maybe that psychology stuff worked in reverse, and perhaps Boog had me psyched. But I never recall making a really good pitch against him. Everything I ever threw to him was right down the chute.

Because of him, the whole Baltimore club hit me pretty well. Even when I won thirty-one games, the Orioles gave me half my six losses. I gave up more home runs against them, had a higher earned run average and beat them only twice all season long. No other team beat me more than once, and five teams couldn't beat me at all!

Now I'll make a confession that doesn't make me swell with pride. I deliberately threw at two hitters in my baseball career. Missed one and hit one. The man I hit was Boog Powell, and I'm convinced that my hitting him in 1968 won the pennant for the Tigers. The race was close and Powell was killing me, so I threw at him. The ball hit his finger and broke it, and put him out of the lineup.

The other guy I threw at was Max Alvis. The Cleveland club was kicking the crap out of me; I was five or six runs behind and it was only the third or fourth inning and I was having a miserable time. My rhythm was off and I couldn't do anything right, and I got mad. Alvis just happened to be the next batter standing up there when my temper got the best of me, and I threw right at his head. There was nothing personal involved, because Max was an all right dude—it's just that I was so mad at myself that the next guy in the batter's box could have been a blind man in a wheelchair and I probably would have thrown at him.

I remember the pitch, even the count. I had him no balls and two strikes. It was the only time I was ahead of a hitter all day and I turned loose a fast ball right for his cap. It was the greatest knock-down pitch I've ever seen.

Somehow Max got out of the way, and when he picked himself up he turned to plate umpire Nestor Chylak and said, "You and I both know he threw at me."

0

"Right. We both know that, Maxie. But with the shit he's throwing today, he couldn't hurt you."

Nestor had a great sense of humor and he's always been a great umpire. Probably the best ball-and-strikes man in the game. I always liked Emmet Ashford, too—he was the first black man to make it to the majors. He used to laugh at some of the crap I'd pull out there on the mound and he had a great sense of humor.

Some umpires don't.

Ashford thought the game was fun, and he made it fun for the players and fans, too, although I guess some of the stuffed shirts in baseball didn't like him. The game needs excitement and Ashford provided it. But one day he got so excited during a game in Minnesota he cost me a home run. Killebrew hit one down the line in left and it had to be twenty feet foul when it went over the fence. Emmet was jumping up and down at third base, yelling foul and pointing fair. Killebrew kept coming around the bases and Ashford wouldn't change his decision and that run beat me.

Ed Hurley was the most shameful excuse for an umpire I ever saw. He seemed to be mad at the world all the time, and he loved to exercise his authority. He umpired one of the first games I pitched in 1964 and we were playing the Angels on the West Coast and Joe Adcock was the hitter.

I quickly got two strikes on him, then threw two pitches that were perfect—low and outside, definitely getting the corner. Hurley called them both balls and I was steaming. So was Freehan and he rarely complains. I rushed to the plate and demanded to know what was wrong with the pitches.

"They were balls and I called them balls, McLain," he yelled. "Your job is to pitch, not to challenge my judgment."

I didn't bother trying to hit the corner with the next pitch. I had runners on second and third with two out and I decided to challenge Adcock with my best fast ball, right down the center of the plate. And that's where I put it, I swear to God.

I'll be damned if Hurley didn't call it ball three. Adcock himself couldn't believe it.

It's the first time I really swore at an umpire, and I was jumping up and down and screaming at Hurley. And he was shouting right back at me. I couldn't believe what he said next.

"Wherever the next one is, McLain, you can be sure it'll be ball four."

I threw another perfect strike and he called it ball four. I

O

went absolutely bananas. I think I'd have strangled him, but Charlie Dressen took me out of the game before I could get my hands on him.

John Rice was another incompetent umpire, and so was John Flaherty. Rice was fat, with a big belly, and he couldn't see over his belly, so you knew there was no way you were going to get the low strike. As for Flaherty, he just got old and couldn't see. He was a supernice gentleman, but simply too old for the game.

Ed Runge was an outstanding umpire and he detested hitters who constantly bitched at him. It's generally true that the truly outstanding players rarely bitch at the umpires, and they have a mutual respect for each other.

Pete Ward of the White Sox was a player who was constantly complaining to the umpires and one game I fanned him four times on just twelve pitches with Runge umpiring. Some of the pitches weren't exactly strikes, but apparently Runge had endured all of Ward's griping that he could and decided to pay him back.

Umpires are human, too. And they liked working games that I pitched, because I worked quickly and they knew it'd be a quick contest.

I remember being thrown out of just two games in the major leagues, and Art Frantz threw me out both times. I was pitching for the Washington Senators and Frantz didn't give me a perfect strike that would have gotten me out of an inning. It was the sixth or seventh inning and I hadn't given up a hit. I was halfway to the dugout when he decided the pitch was a ball.

I fumed a little then, but went back to pitching. Sure as hell, I hit someone in the small of the back, gave up a couple of hits, and suddenly I'm losing a game that I had in my hip pocket. When the inning was finally over, I walked to the plate and started calling Frantz every name in the book. "One more word and you're out of the game," he warned.

I couldn't resist, so I told him, "One more word."

I was out of there, just like he promised.

About a month later he was umpiring one of our games in Oakland against the Athletics and he called a balk on me. I've never balked in my life! All I wanted was for him to explain to me what I did wrong.

"I can't explain it, McLain, but you made a kind of funny move toward third base and I'm calling it a balk."

0

Jesus, Mary, and Joseph! Here's a major league umpire calling a balk and he can't explain it! I did my full bananas number, kicking dirt and raging around like a wounded water buffalo. I bumped him with my chest, like Leo Durocher used to do, but he took that. He turned and went back to brush off home plate, and I walked up and kicked dirt on it again. Still he didn't throw me out.

What did it were the magic words "mother fucker."

Or is that one word?

Whatever, I was out of there.

Still, I really don't dislike Art, and I think all in all I enjoyed a pretty good relationship with the umpires. The one thing a pitcher has to do is study the umpires almost as thoroughly as he does the enemy batters, because umpires work differently. Some will give you the high strike, or the low one—and some won't. Every one works a game a little differently, and you're pitching for them as well as to the batter and your catcher.

I got very apprehensive when I faced a batter who always gave me fits. I was never scared pitching, but I think the word "apprehensive" is the right one. I was afraid of making a mistake, so as a consequence I pitched too carefully and made even bigger mistakes than I would have normally.

Giving up a home run never bothered me as much as giving up a walk. I just hated to walk a batter. I guess it's true that I pretty much dared batters to hit me, and challenged them with my best stuff, especially when I was ahead in the game. One season, I gave up forty home runs, but twenty-seven of them were with no one on base, so they didn't hurt for the most part.

Look at it this way—what's tougher to pitch out of, a one-run home run or a whole bunch of singles? A home run is one run, and it's a clean one. Carl Yastrzemski and Boog Powell and Reggie Jackson and the rest have hit some balls off me that probably are still in orbit. But home runs that didn't cost us a game never really bothered me.

I've heard for years that guys would win without their good stuff and lose when they had it. I've had experiences like that, but for the most part if you have your good stuff working you'll win, and if you don't they're gonna kick the daylights out of you. It's really a very simple thing with no great mystery to it. The only time in my career I had consistently good stuff and lost was in Washington, because we simply couldn't score any runs.

A while back I touched on this matter of my being a slow

starter, and throughout my career I never really popped the ball until the third or fourth inning. If my problem were simply a muscular one, I'd have warmed up longer, or gotten a rub-down, or something. But the soreness was so deep that I really was afraid to cut loose with the ball until I knew I was loose.

So I had to be more of a pitcher in the early innings. I had to really know where to put the ball, and when to change speeds. Later on, when I got loose, I could let it rip. The batters must have been terribly confused at times and it may have seemed to them I was really two different pitchers. In reality, I was—a guy who tried to finesse the ball around in the early stages and one who tried to jam it into their bats when I got loose.

The one thing I had going for me, no matter what, was the confidence that I could win. Other pitchers surely had more natural stuff—on our staff in 1968 Daryl Patterson had wonder-ful stuff but never materialized and Joe Sparma had tremen-dous velocity but lacked something—but no one had more belief in himself than I did. One of the finest compliments I ever got was from one of our coaches, Wally Moses, who called me "the greatest competitor between the lines I've ever seen. The man just oozes the fire of competition."

And that's the truth. I loved all of it, especially that personal duel with the batter, and the better the batter, the more I wanted to win. I know I sometimes was probably careless with the lesser hitters and didn't bear down as I should have. But you can't bear down all the time and anyone who thinks you can is an idiot.

Control is 80 percent of pitching. There are guys winning twenty every year who don't have a great anything—no super-fast ball, no snapping curve, and no great any pitch—but they have just enough stuff, and they win because they can move the baseball in and out, up and down. Catfish Hunter and Andy Messersmith are two good examples of this kind of pitching. Gaylord Perry, too, although he has the world's greatest spitter.

Mel Stottlemyre is a dandy pitcher because he keeps the ball low and the batters keep pounding the ball into the ground. Joel Horlen and Gary Peters won for years on prac-tically nothing but good control (although Horlen had a fine spitter, too), and Tom Seaver, although blessed with an out-standing fast ball, wins because he has great control of his pitches.

Jim Kaat has been a consistent winner over the years be-

0

cause he has always been much more than just a thrower. I mean, the man knew what he was doing when he stepped out there on the field. He had good information on the hitters, and that's a big part of the game.

If you're going to make a decent living by pitching, it's not enough to have good stuff and good control—you simply have to take enough of an interest to try to understand what pitching is all about. The ball and bat are so lively that a one-armed cheerleader can knock the thing into the stands, and it's more important than ever for a pitcher to study the guys who are trying to make a living at his expense.

I laughed a lot, I had fun, and I even talked with opposing players. But between the foul lines, I concentrated on my job. I had intense concentration, as a matter of fact. I tried not to hear a thing, although sometimes you can't help it. If you lose your concentration, you lose your control.

Old Frank Lary used to kill the New York Yankees and he did very well against the other good teams like Boston and Cleveland when the Indians were strong. But he just sort of shuffled along in games against the lower clubs like Kansas City and Washington in those days. No one ever came up with the reason why. All they ever came up with was a silly little nickname, The Yankee Killer.

I saw Frank just briefly, but the explanation is simple. He beat the Yankees for two reasons: He thought he could beat them, and they thought he could beat them.

Hell, he just didn't *think* he could win when he pitched against them, he *knew* he could. And every time he beat them, both he and the Yankee hitters would be even more convinced of his invincibility.

Now we're talking about concentration, we're talking about confidence and we're talking about the psychology of the game, that man-to-man combat between pitcher and batter.

Wilt Chamberlain will never admit it, but that's why Bill Russell owned his fanny, because Russell knew in his heart he could handle Wilt, and it got so that Wilt knew it, too.

Sure, I challenged hitters, I dared them to hit the ball, but never once in my major league career did I do that with a chance of losing the game. With a two- or three-run lead, sure, I'd pretty much say, "Here it comes, asshole, try and hit it."

But contrary to popular belief, I didn't do any challenging of that sort when things were close, when I could get whipped. When I went into the seventh inning with the lead, no one was

0

going to win that game but me. I had a pretty good fast ball, a fine change-up, and an average curve, and I knew what to do with them. I wasn't just some clown who wound up and threw the ball anywhere. Most of the time, I had a pretty good idea where it was going.

God gave me the fast ball, Charlie Dressen taught me how to throw the curve, and Johnny Sain helped me throw a slider. I had almost as much trouble learning to throw the slider as I had with the curve. I tried just about everything.

My good fast ball was straight overhand with my fingers across the seams. When I wanted to throw it sidearm, I threw it with the seams. Sain taught me to grip the slider exactly the same way as the fast ball except to hold it off center a bit—then you actually cut the ball and if you do it right, the ball will slide about three or four inches and dip down a bit.

Sain worked with me all of 1967, but not until May of 1968 did I perfect it. One day, it just started working.

My change-up is a pitch I couldn't teach anybody else how to throw because it's difficult even to explain. When I turned the ball loose—with the same grip and motion as my fast ball—I sort of flopped my shoulder and the ball changed up. Sain also taught me what he called the running change-up where you get the feeling that you're almost carrying the ball up to the hitter. Technically it's a balk because you don't release the ball when the rules say you must, but an umpire never catches it.

I never developed the knack for throwing the spitball, but hundreds of pitchers have and the umpires damn well know it.

Why baseball doesn't legalize the spitter I'll never know. Every rule put into baseball in the last fifty years has been designed to benefit the hitter. What about the poor pitcher?

Forget the old bullshit about the spitball being unsanitary. What's so damned clean about chewing tobacco? Baseball isn't running a contest for *House Beautiful*.

The rules committee of baseball is living in the Dark Ages and is made up of men who know precious little about modern day baseball. The next thing they'll want the pitchers to concede is the secrecy of the next pitch.

Everyone knows Gaylord Perry owns the game's finest spitter. Ronnie Kline used to have a dandy one, and some of my old Tiger teammates, Mickey Lolich and Phil Regan, had the spitter working pretty well. John Wyatt did, too, except he used Preparation H instead of saliva.

Like I said, I never could throw it, but the spitball takes a tremendous drop—and I don't mean just a couple of inches. Perry's spitball is like a marble falling off a tabletop. Lew Burdette must have had a pretty good one in his time because he was working with the Atlanta pitchers when I was there, trying to get them to throw it correctly. It's a most difficult pitch to learn. But once you have it, you actually have two weapons— the actual pitch, and the thought that's in the batter's mind that you're apt to throw it all the time.

It's pretty much a two-strike pitch that you use when you have to get a man out. The only time I ever tried a spitter in a game was against the Angels, and Phil Regan had been working with me to try to teach me how to throw the thing. I figured if Joel Horlen could throw it every other pitch and guys like Jim Lonborg and Juan Pizarro and Jim Perry and Jim Kaat could do it, there was no reason I couldn't.

Jim Fregosi was the hitter and I had two strikes on him when I decided on the big unveiling. Jimmy's a good friend of mine and a fine hitter, but I've always been able to get him out and he knows it.

There were two out, and two on, and we had a 2–0 lead. The simple thing was to give Jim another fast ball to his blind spot and go to the bench, but the temptation to throw this magnificent new pitch was too much to resist.

The first problem I had was that when I loaded up my hand with saliva and got ready to throw the ball, it looked like a cloudburst had hit my hand. The baseball was so slippery it was all I could do to hold onto it.

Fregosi hit it nine miles. Next morning in the papers when he was asked what kind of pitch he had hit, he said, "I don't know, I think that pitch came out of a thunderstorm."

From that minute on, I decided to leave the spitter to the experts.

I never could understand why Sam McDowell fooled around with the spitter, either. Here was the finest left-handed pitcher I've ever seen, and he starts tinkering around with that pitch when he already has the finest fast ball and the best curve in the business. All Sam had to do was adjust his mental outlook on the game. In fact, he had so much ability he probably could have gotten along with no outlook at all. Just go out there and throw the damned thing and think about nothing at all.

I've always felt it was such a terrible waste, and that if someone could have drummed some common sense into him,

0

Sam McDowell could have been a better pitcher than Sandy Koufax.

I can't read a man's mind, but I always wondered down deep inside me if Sam McDowell really loved the competition, the confrontation, as much as I did. I loved to pitch even when I was almost ready to drop from fatigue and exhaustion, as I often was in 1968 and 1969 when I was trying to do so many things and trying to cover up the crap in my life like a cat covering its droppings.

Only once can I recall actually asking to be taken out of a game. It was in 1969 and I had a 5–0 lead and was about to drop right there on the mound. Little wonder.

I had been up for two nights, flying people around the country in one of our jet planes. We were on a home stand, and the business was too good to turn down. So I flew from Detroit to Denver to Wichita, dropped off my passenger (who incidentally never knew I was anybody except a private jet pilot), and then went to Chicago to pick up my cousin who was going to sit with our kids that weekend while Sharyn went on part of a road trip with me.

After flying all night and all morning, I finally landed back in Detroit at two thirty in the afternoon. Then I had two meetings before going to the ball park at six.

When we got the 5–0 lead, I signaled for Mayo Smith to come out to the mound, and I told him to get somebody warmed up because I was about to faint. By the time he got someone ready, it was 5–3 with two on and two out. He had Dick Radatz and Fred Lasher warming up and told me he was going to bring Radatz in to bail me out of trouble.

We stood on the mound and argued about it. I told him pretty much what was on my mind.

"Jesus Christ, Mayo, Radatz is a good friend of mine but he hasn't gotten anybody out since 1966. Lasher was your best man in the bullpen last season."

Mayo was in no mood to argue.

"It's gonna be Radatz, Denny."

"Then, by God, I ain't leavin' this game."

Well, that's a bunch of shit, too, because it was Mayo's second trip to the mound in that inning and under the rules somebody has to leave, and it was me. By this time, Radatz is taking the baseball and he's cockier than hell.

"Who's the hitter?"

Mayo tells him. "Hawk Taylor."

O

"Shit, just relax, Mayo. I own this asshole."

"Don't forget to pitch him low."

Those were Mayo's only instructions and we had gotten into a big argument in the clubhouse over Hawk Taylor when we were going over the other team's hitters. Two or three veteran pitchers had argued with Mayo that Taylor was a good low ball hitter and that we should pitch him up high if he got into the game.

But Mayo's orders were to pitch him low, and Radatz did just that. He fed him a fast ball down around his ankles, and Taylor hit it into outer space and we blew the game 6–5.

By the time the ball sailed out of sight, I was in the clubhouse listening to the game on radio and I ripped all the buttons off my shirt. I was plenty mad, but not as mad as Radatz. He came in swearing, "Fuck Mayo Smith. What a dumb shit."

The next week Radatz was in Toledo and Hawk Taylor was still striking out on high ones and hitting low ones out of the park.

Ask Mayo Smith today what he thinks of me and I'll venture he says he has a good feeling about me and loved me as a competitor—and I have good feelings about him as a manager. But we hammered away at each other every once in a while, even after we had settled those differences back in 1967.

One time in 1969 I was struggling along, throwing the ball almost everywhere but over the plate, but somehow in the seventh inning I was managing to hold onto a 3–0 lead. I hadn't walked a lot of batters, but I took almost everyone to a three-and-two count and I must have thrown 140 pitches. I don't even remember the team we were playing, but I had the bases loaded and not a soul out and Mayo comes strolling out of the dugout.

"I'm taking you out."

"You'll have to beat the shit out of me to get me out of this game."

I guess I had been in so much trouble that night, and had gotten out without a run being scored against me, that I thought I'd like to try once more. It's one of those situations every pitcher would like to think he thrives on.

"Denny, this just doesn't make sense."

"Mayo, you've stuck with me all through 1968 and you know you don't have another soul in the bullpen you can count on. Goddamn it, let me finish what I've started."

0

We agreed that if anyone got a base hit, I'd come out.

No one did, but someone nearly took Don Wert's hand off with a line drive at third, Norm Cash stabbed a vicious liner at first, then Al Kaline made a diving catch of a little looper in right and we got out of it.

Simple. Just like I knew what I was doing.

It's like I've always said, give me five or six runs and fielders who aren't afraid to stand in front of line drives and I'll win most of the time for you.

One of the all-time funniest incidents happened one night against Baltimore. As usual, the Orioles were eating me alive. As I recall, Don Buford and Davey Johnson started the game with singles, Frank Robinson drove one between third and short and Boog Powell doubled off the wall in right. It's 3–0, there's no one out and the game isn't three minutes old and here comes Mayo.

"What the hell is going on?"

"What do you mean?" I asked. "Mayo, if you're not watching, old buddy, you're missing one helluva game."

He had a sense of humor but it didn't surface then. I wasn't happy about the situation, either, but I couldn't very well slash my wrists in front of 45,000 people.

"Denny, you're not doing very well."

"No shit, Mayo." He always was the master of understatement.

"I mean it, Denny. This shit's gotta stop or I'm gonna make a pitching change."

"Wait a minute, Mayo, you can't do that. Hell, I'm not even warmed up yet."

"How's your arm?"

"Fine."

"How's your elbow?"

"Fine."

"And your shoulder?"

"Fine."

"Then what the hell is bothering you?"

"Nothing is bothering me, damn it, I'm just not loose yet but I feel pretty good."

"Well then, how's your stuff?"

Now that's no question to ask a pitcher, who naturally is prejudiced, so I told him, "Mayo, you can't ask me a question like that. Why don't you ask Freehan?"

Bill had been standing on the mound with us and up to

0

then hadn't uttered a word. So Mayo turned to him and said, "Well, how's his stuff?"

"How the hell would I know? I haven't caught anything yet."

Mayo immediately broke up. He was laughing so hard I thought he would fall off the mound.

Right away he jerked me from the game. He had a sense of humor, all right, but what he was seeing that night was anything but funny. For me, it was funny then despite the fact I was getting the manure kicked out of me and it's even funnier now looking back on it.

Later that same season we were playing the Twins in Minnesota and the game was being nationally televised by NBC. Norm Cash was having a great day. He was four-for-four and I was pitching a 5–0 shutout going into the top of the ninth.

It didn't take a genius to figure out that either Norm Cash or Dennis Dale McLain would be the hero of the day, and thus the guest on the postgame show on NBC, and thus the lucky recipient of a crisp new fifty-dollar bill. It wasn't the end of the world, but it was enough to get you through a long, cold night in Minnesota.

As we came to bat in the ninth, Cash was the fourth hitter and he didn't particularly care to come to bat again since he could protect his perfect day. Jim Merritt was pitching and he got the first two batters out, then walked someone so Cash had to come up. And I started yelling from the dugout.

"Hook him. Change-up on him. He can't hit anything low and away."

I knew if he got Cash out, and I preserved my shutout, I'd get the money.

Merritt fanned Norman on three pitches.

As I walked toward the mound, Cash went by me on his way to his position and muttered, "You motherfucker, make sure they don't hit it toward first base. If they do, anything near me is a sure double and they'll score. They might even beat you if they hit two my way."

I got the first two batters on popups to the shortstop.

Tony Oliva, a mighty tough hitter, was next up, but I got him to hit a slider back to the mound. I picked up the ball and looked to first and Cash was just standing in his normal position, about fifteen feet from the base. He had that big shit-eating grin all over his Texas face, so I had to run like hell to beat Oliva to the bag for the third out.

0

I got the shutout, the appearance on the postgame show and the fifty-dollar fee.

When I returned to the clubhouse, I pasted the fifty bucks on my forehead and walked right past Norm's locker.

"Fuck you, McLain," he mumbled.

Norman was one of our better ad libbers.

A LOT OF VULTURES

12

AND A FEW PUSSYCATS

I don't suppose I'll ever totally understand the press (and when I say press, I'm talking about newspapers, magazines, television and radio people, you name it) and I have what you might call a love-hate relationship with the people involved. Like anyone else, I enjoy good publicity, and I detest the bad. Anyone who tells you he enjoys bad publicity is one of your larger dummies.

Basically, I've had more respect for people in television and radio because it's pretty tough to misquote someone on tape or on film. From the very beginning of my career, I gave all of them something to say, something to write about. I liked the limelight from the outset, and to make no bones about it, I capitalized on the press and its interest in me. I never wanted to be just another face in the crowd. Even in high school, I enjoyed reading the things people said about me.

For a long time, all of it was good, and maybe in my early days I thought that all writers were my friends, that they were cheerleaders, or camp followers of a sort. As a matter of fact, many of them are. They fall in love with athletes who have skills they never had, who can do things they only dreamed of doing, and they're in a sort of seventh heaven when their man is doing well.

Let him stumble, though, and they're like vultures. Not all of them, mind you, but some of them. They pick at your carcass because you've disappointed them.

Never mind that you have disappointed yourself, or your family, or your teammates.

I gave all of them something to write and I enjoyed it. They had a job to do and I loved to give them copy. But as I matured, I learned that they have their weaknesses too, and that some of them are nothing more than hero-worshippers hugging the coattails of the athletes. They have their own problems and their own hangups and their own personal miseries, and more than once in a while those things manifest themselves in their columns and stories.

One incident illustrates the basic difference between me and the athlete who's scared of the front office and afraid of controversy. When the Tigers fired Johnny Sain as pitching coach, I said publicly it was "a big mistake."

Mickey Lolich, on the other hand, said: "If I said what I think, I'd get in trouble with the front office."

Lolich is the same spoiled kid he's always been. When I

0

was sitting out the 1970 opener because of my suspension and Lolich won the game, he remarked to newsmen who had gathered around his locker, "I'll tell you one thing, if McLain was here and available right now you guys wouldn't be talking to me."

Isn't that childish?

And the headline in Pete Waldmeir's column in *The Detroit News* that afternoon was "McLain Manages to Upstage Tigers, Lolich On Opening Day."

My upstaging consisted of showing up at a meeting with Commissioner Bowie Kuhn, so he could inform me how he expected me to conduct myself during my suspension. President Nixon made a belated appearance at the opening game in Washington that day too. Was he deliberately upstaging Lolich?

Waldmeir spent several years of his career trying to embarrass me. He need not have done that; I did enough to embarrass myself. But he was guilty of inaccurate reporting on more than one occasion. He and I had a long conversation one evening about the Detroit fans. I was upset because they had booed Al Kaline, and I stung the fans pretty good for that. I just couldn't understand how the people of that town could boo a man who had given them so much enjoyment for so many years.

I was talking about a small percentage of the fans, certainly not all of them, and I made that very clear to Pete. But that wasn't the way it was written. It came out that I had put the rip on *all* the Tiger fans, calling them ". . . front runners, the worst in the league. I could care less what they think."

The fans, generally, have been very kind to me and my family, and I certainly wouldn't blast all of them because some idiot planted a smoke bomb in my wife's car and scared the daylights out of her on the way to the airport. I couldn't blame all the Tiger fans because a couple of them behind the Tiger dugout yelled obscenities at me and asked me things like "Denny, who are you betting on tonight?"

Ninety-five percent of the mail I've received over the years has been favorable, so I'm convinced that the great majority of the fans, not only in Detroit but everywhere else, are good folks. But the other five percent are horseshit, make no mistake about that.

When I pitched my first major league victory, the stories

were good, and I remember them. Jerry Green, then with the Associated Press, wrote that I had "the poise of a veteran." I didn't, but it was nice of him to write that.

Watson Spoelstra, who later was to get a bucket of water on his head, allowed as how I pitched myself ". . . into the 1964 strategy of the Detroit Tigers."

Pretty heady stuff for a kid of nineteen.

That was just the beginning. Better headlines came later:

McLAIN AHEAD OF TIME

McLAIN RAGS TO RICHES STORY

DENNY FINDS PLACE IN SUN

DENNY SHRUGS OFF PRESSURE

MORE GLORY AWAITING DENNY

McLAIN GOOD BET FOR ALL-STAR GAME

McLAIN SUPERB

McLAIN EARNS CASEY'S PRAISE

McLAIN CLASSY FLINGER

McLAIN PASSES TEST FOR MOUND GREATNESS

McLAIN BIG MAN IN MARKET PLACE, TOO

DENNY GETS NO. 30

I was on the cover of *Time.* Columnists from all parts of the country were following me around. I was on every television network. I had more offers than I could handle, from Vegas to Viet Nam.

You want me to tell you I didn't enjoy it? That I disliked the press? No way, not when the headlines were good.

But when my life turned sour, so did they, and I wasn't mature enough to handle that, either. It hit me hard when I got the short end of the publicity. I got to a point where I could understand the bad publicity that I had coming to me, but to this day I cannot comprehend the vicious attacks, the one-sided, the slanted, and the malicious lies.

Take the celebrated account of the McLain-Lolich fiasco at the all-star game in Washington in 1969. The whole thing was bizarre. It was written in such a way as to paint me as one who had abandoned a child (I guess in some ways I had) or who went around kicking dogs and little kids.

0

Both Mickey Lolich and I were selected for the American League team. About a week before the game, he asked if I planned to fly my own plane to Washington. I told him yes, and he asked if he and his wife, Joyce, could ride along.

I said sure, even though Mickey never was one of my favorite people. He had nothing I wanted, but obviously I had some things he wanted, like a lot of national attention. There were five of us including our wives and my pilot, Bill Bollinger.

Mickey asked about my return plans. I informed him I had to be back in Detroit first thing Wednesday morning for a dental appointment, since I was having extensive reconstruction work done on my teeth.

The all-star game was scheduled for Tuesday night, but when we got to the park there was the threat of rain. Lolich wanted to know about my plans in the event of rain. I reminded him that no matter what, I simply had to be in Detroit the next morning for dental work, and that on Thursday I had an urgent meeting in Florida.

"You'd better make your own plans for getting back to Detroit if we have rain tonight," I told him.

We had rain. Tons of it. The game was rescheduled for the following night, so Sharyn and I and our pilot hopped in the six-seater plane and headed back to Detroit. Next morning I was in the dentist's chair for several hours and we decided to take the Lear jet back to Washington. My dentist went with us; he even did some cleaning work on my teeth while we were in the air.

Back in Washington late that afternoon at the clubhouse, Mickey asked for the umpteenth time about my travel plans. Again I told him I was leaving as soon as I pitched because of my pressing business engagements. And he knew he'd have to wait around for nine innings, or at least until he got into the game and finished his performance. I pitched one inning, gave up a run, a hit, struck out a couple, and was gone.

The following day in Florida, I got word that Mickey had come up with a big sob story in the Detroit papers about how an inconsiderate Denny McLain had stranded him and his wife in Washington.

It was not only a lie, but it was a gutless thing to do. Lolich lacked the courage to confront anyone face-to-face when he had a gripe, but he wasn't at all hesitant about popping off to the press. And the press didn't bother to check with me as to the accuracy of the story before blasting out.

0

Did the press report that I hadn't charged Mickey a thin dime for the trip to Washington, and that he was reimbursed for his round trip ticket? You bet your sweet ass no one reported that.

And here's a guy who told one of our coaches on the night I came back after my suspension that he'd be rooting against the Tigers for the first time in his life. And he's the same guy who complained that attention was drawn away from his pitching by Al Kaline's pursuit of the three thousand-hit plateau. What a childish thing to say!

But then, nobody's perfect.

Lolich has been the darling of the Detroit press corps, yet he doesn't have a close friend on the ball club. And from the beginning of his career, he's complained bitterly about the team not getting enough runs for him. He's just not one of the guys, and it's a shame because the good Lord blessed him with a magnificent arm. Too bad his head doesn't work as well.

He even had his attorney call me and demand a $2,000 fee to take part in a tennis tournament for charity! We finally had to give him $1,500 because he had given his tentative okay, we had advertised he'd be there. Then he had the balls to have his lawyer call again and ask us for a letter saying that Mickey was donating the money to charity.

The man's only charity is in his own hip pocket, and when it comes to money, he's a lot like some writers—they have fishhooks in one pocket and flypaper in the other and they never pull out any money to pick up any tabs.

Lolich and Bill Freehan were liberally quoted—and Freehan wrote it in his book—that the Tigers had one set of rules for Denny McLain and another set for the other twenty-four players. They intimated that I didn't bother to show up some of the time.

None of the writers went to Manager Mayo Smith to ask him about these accusations, and the truth is that I was never away from the club without Mayo's permission. The only time I ever came close to missing a game was one occasion when we were playing in Cleveland and I had been in the hospital in Detroit for treatment of phlebitis.

I had pitched in Cleveland on Sunday (and won, incidentally) and Mayo knew I was hurting. It was Mayo who suggested I return to Detroit and check into the hospital for a couple of days of treatment. So I spent Monday, Tuesday, and Wednesday getting treatments at Ford Hospital, and got out Thursday

0

morning for the trip back to Cleveland. I was to pitch that night. Mayo had phoned me at the hospital and asked if I would be able to start. I told him yes.

We flew our own plane to Cleveland but when we got out over Lake Erie, we noticed a high exhaust temperature reading. I turned back and returned to City Airport so a mechanic could check it out. By the time we got things repaired, it was nip-and-tuck whether I'd make it to Cleveland in time for the game. I got into the clubhouse at 7:10 P.M., twenty minutes ahead of game time, had precious little time to warm up, and took the mound in the bottom of the first, not certain that I had my fly closed.

The Indians hit rockets in the first three innings while I was getting warmed up, but they always hit them at someone. We won the game 4–0, and later in his book Freehan made the comment that despite everything else about me, ". . . when he comes to the park he's ready to pitch."

No one bothered to check with Mayo about the Cleveland incident, while some of my teammates were making jokes about "Sky King" circling the stadium (which was a lie), just as no one bothered to check the facts on the all-star game incident, when in fact I did have permission of my manager, and he in turn had the permission of American League President Joe Cronin for me to return to Detroit for my dental work.

But some people in the media operate with the theory that one should never let the truth stand in the way of a good story. There was enough about me that was bad and truthful. No one ever needed to resort to untruths to get an interesting story.

When things like the Lolich incident started happening, I began to wonder about my relationship with the press. I know, and Lolich knows, that when I left Washington there were no hard feelings. He knew the deal and he understood it. Still, there were big headlines in the Detroit papers. As soon as I got the word, I called General Manager Jim Campbell and sounded off. When I got back to Detroit, I talked with Mayo Smith about it and told him I had to talk to Lolich to get it off my chest. So I asked Mickey to come into the old uniform storage room down the hall from the locker room and I let him know exactly how I felt. The language I used wasn't the Sunday-school type.

Naturally, Lolich said he had been misquoted, and that he probably had popped off a bit because he was mad that he didn't get to pitch earlier in the game. I demanded an apology. I got a lame one, and the papers buried it on page seventy-five.

You think that ended it? No way, O'Shea.

0

Next time I went out to pitch in Tiger Stadium, I got the hell booed out of me—because the fans took the first story that was so prominently displayed and believed it, while they ignored the apology. And that, basically, is one of the things wrong with the press today.

There's the old adage about bad news traveling fast. Well, it's always helped out by small-minded people anxious to bury someone who's in trouble. The late Doc Greene was fair to me. In his columns in *The Detroit News,* Doc ripped me when I had it coming and praised me when praise was due, but he was always fair. Jerry Green was on the story much of the time, and he started following my career when he was with AP. He was writing for *The Detroit News* by the time I got to the top, and I have to say that although I got disgusted seeing him around all the time when I was trying to hide, he was fair in his approach. I don't think he ever deliberately went out of his way to hurt me, and I never got the idea he was chuckling to himself when my troubles mounted.

Others were downright sick in their posture. I could almost see them clapping their hands as the storm clouds swelled around my head.

Let's investigate the investigators!

Doug Mintline of the Flint *Journal* once wrote that he had witnessed me making bets and had duly reported that alleged fact to Manager Mayo Smith and General Manager Jim Campbell, but that they had chosen not to do anything about it.

How the hell does he know I was making a bet? Did he have the telephone tapped?

On the other hand, Pete Sark, a radio broadcaster and writer in Flint, has bent over backwards over the years to help me tell my side of the story. He hasn't hidden any awful truths about me, yet he hasn't gone off half-cocked and spread any lies, either.

Edwin Pope of the Miami *Herald* had written some pretty strong things against me, and while I was living in Florida I followed his column avidly. One time I got so upset at some of the things he was saying I popped off about him to a friend.

"He's a terrific guy, Denny, you oughta get to know him."

So we arranged to meet about a week later, and we hit it off right away. He followed us around for a round of golf, we had lunch, and he wound up writing a very nice article about me. We saw something in each other that we didn't know ex-

0

isted prior to our meeting, and since then he's been fair with me. Tough, but fair. And that's all I ask.

David Condon of the Chicago *Tribune* is another writer who's played it right down the middle. He's been on me when I was wrong and behind me when I was right. You just can't ask for anything nicer than that.

One of my favorite characters of all time is Bernie Cohen, a field producer for ABC News. He's done dozens of stories on me for network television and not all favorable stories, I might add. I never liked it when I saw myself being talked about by some federal official or when I saw the commissioner reading a statement expelling me from baseball. But here again, we get back to my attempt to understand the job responsible journalists have to do. Naturally, Bernie wanted a scoop now and again and he wanted good quotes, and because of his tremendous fairness, I gave both things to him every now and again.

Only once did we hassle. He had followed me to Florida after the first suspension, and he was determined to get an interview. I was just as determined to say nothing, because I was under orders to keep my mouth shut. And, much as I wanted to do this favor for Bernie, I just couldn't accommodate him. Bernie was mad for a while, but he got over it when I bought him dinner. In that respect, Bernie is a lot like other media folks. He's pretty snug with the bucks.

I had barely gotten settled into my routine in Florida when I was victimized again by some terribly malicious reporting. I was keeping busy with golf and tennis, trying to stay in shape for my return to the baseball wars.

One afternoon, my foursome just completed the eighth hole and we were walking off the green. My partner, Don O'Malley, was already in the golf cart waiting for me. I was fifty or sixty feet away from him and I swung my putter like a tennis racquet, just horsing around. I wasn't mad at anybody. How could I be? I had just birdied the hole.

But the head of the putter flew off and hit my friend O'Malley square in the mouth. He bled profusely. Some teeth were shattered. We got him to the clubhouse and there stood a reporter from an Orlando television station.

You can imagine the story that went out.

"Denny McLain in Trouble Again"

From there it got worse. There were stories that it was a temper tantrum, that we had argued on the golf course, that there was a hassle over betting, you name it. It was just awful.

I've thrown a few clubs in my time and I'm not the most placid person you'll meet, but this club was not thrown. It was an accident, pure and simple. I've never been sorrier for anything in my life, and it's a terrible feeling when you've hurt a good friend. I'd never in my life do anything to hurt Don O'Malley, who's been one of the most steadfast of my friends.

But the media didn't see it that way, simply because the media didn't care to look for the truth.

At this stage of my life, almost every headline was scary, almost every story unfavorable.

McLAIN FILES FOR BANKRUPTCY

DENNY SUSPENDED

DENNY SUSPENDED AGAIN

GOOD OL' DENNY . . . HE DID IT AGAIN

DENNY'S TRAGEDY: HE'S DESTROYING HIS CAREER

DENNY'S BUSINESS VENTURES IN TANGLED STATE

DENNY KAYOED AGAIN

McLAIN'S FAST BALL GONE

Like 'em? I hated all of them, and I couldn't control anything. It was all downhill.

No one is ever fully prepared for bad publicity. I've tried to rationalize it and tell myself that even a man who's elected President of the United States has millions and millions of folks who not only vote against him, but who hate his guts. I'm sorry, but that knowledge doesn't help me. I want people to like me, even though I realize the things I've done haven't always been designed to win friends and influence people.

I was upset by the reviews for my nightclub act in Las Vegas that I put on after the World Series:

"Uncomfortable and self-conscious, he put on an opening exhibition incredibly naive and static. His keyboarding on the organ is monotonous. . . . pugnacious and even insolent at times with loungers and toward his musicians, McLain also reveals extraordinarily bad taste in warbling a stag lyric. . . . fortunately, it's his only attempt at singing. . . . he needs to discipline himself plenty for this kind of showcasing and, if he does that, plus stepping down off the mound for a while, he might become an entertainer."

O

You'd have to be an idiot to like that kind of review, even if it did get my name in *Variety.*

Another fellow named Perry Phillips of the Oakland *Tribune* reviewed the very same act—in fact, he stayed for both shows:

"Professional athletes aren't usually good musicians and vice versa. There are exceptions however, and Denny McLain is one of them."

He called me "a pretty darn good organist." He said the opening show was anything but auspicious, described me and my group as nervous (and we were trembling), and referred to our shaky moments. He said one of our parodies was in poor taste, and I realized later it was and dropped it from the second show. He said my attempts at comedy didn't exactly hit the strike zone. Hell, I knew that. I could tell the people weren't splitting their sides with laughter.

But guys like Shecky Greene and Marty Allen were super to me and gave me some good advice. I'll never be a threat to them, but I like to entertain people. We didn't have a top-flight Vegas act and never will, but we were booked there because of the thirty-one-game season and the World Series, and the critics should have understood that.

Booing is an American tradition, but show me a person who likes it and I'll show you a moron. I didn't like it when I was booed in my first start after the Lolich airport incident; I didn't like it when I was booed on opening day of the 1969 season. Here, I had won thirty-one games, the Cy Young Award, the most valuable player award, and when I went out to get my World Series ring, the fans started booing.

When I criticized the fans for getting on Kaline, I was booed the next time I stuck my head out of the dugout.

Fans and writers are alike in one respect: They're fickle. But they're different in that some writers love you to pieces when you're going well and get on your fanny when things sour. The fans in Detroit seemed to ride my fanny when I was going well, but they seemed to rally behind me when all my trouble popped up publicly.

Detroit has a different type of sports fan. It has a lot of good things going for it, but let's face it, Detroit's not a sophisticated city. It's a factory town. It's a blue-collar place. The fans seem to have a closer identification with the player.

They don't go away for weekends, they go to the ballyard. Their release is their favorite sports team, not a yacht or a trip

0

to Acapulco. They live and die with their guys on the field, and they're a hardy group of sometimes rowdy, sometimes hard-drinking and leather-lunged people.

I really didn't understand them when I was playing the game, but having been away from it, I can look at it much more objectively. Maybe some writers and broadcasters should do that—take a couple of years off just to observe. Then they'd be much more aware of the situation.

I'm not saying you have to have played the game to be able to write or talk about it, but I think it's possible that some writers and broadcasters live an unreal existence in that they have no real knowledge of an athlete's mind or makeup.

A classic example of this is Joe Falls of *The Detroit Free Press.*

He'll rip me and this book no matter what I say about him, simply because he's a ripper. He ripped Charlie Dressen even after he was dead and gone, so I know he'll have a field day with me and this book—and all his readers know it, too.

I know Joe Falls a lot better than he knows me. I even know why he's such a negative person. It's because he's miserable all the time. He's a person who knows he's unpopular even with his co-workers, so how the hell could he be positive and uplifting about anything?

But in the early days I was his pet. Let me quote from one of his articles in the glory years, just before the roof caved in: "I had sort of adopted McLain as my special player. We had this bond, see, this mutual respect . . . I felt superior to these Johnny-come-latelys of the journalistic world who were trying to catch up and get the real dope on my boy."

My boy, my ass.

I don't want to spend any more time on him because it's a battle I cannot win. I can't even get a tie out of it, because he'll tear me apart until the day I die—and he'll most likely take a cheap shot at me even then. There's one guy I'd like to put under the same microscope he's used for me and others. Then watch him sweat blood!

There's a guy in Chicago who's been mad at me for years, because I gave him what I thought was a good news scoop and it turned out to be a false alarm. I had heard from what I was convinced were most reliable sources that Billy Martin was coming to Detroit to manage the Tigers after the 1967 season. I told that to a writer in Chicago—and I told him not to quote me.

O

I was just trying to be a good guy, because I honestly believed the Tigers would fire Mayo Smith.

The story backfired, and Martin wasn't hired until some years later, but the writer never forgave me. To this day he thinks I deliberately stiffed him.

Lucky for me the story was erroneous. I never could have played for Billy Martin. He's a ruthless man and I can't stand dictators.

One of the most pleasant men I ever met in the media is Charles Maher of Los Angeles. He came to Birmingham when I was in the minors (on the way out) and took a road trip with us, just to see what life in the minor leagues was like for Denny McLain. I did a full performance for him. Of course, I rarely took buses. I managed to fly to most places, even then. But for Charlie I did it, and it was fun, and the story he wrote was a good one. All he did to make it good was to tell the truth.

I've always admired Jim Murray too, even though he came down pretty hard on me when I was suspended. He's a gifted writer and I enjoy reading his stuff. He's properly irreverent and I get the idea sometimes that he really doesn't care all that much about sports like some writers do. In other words, he's no jock.

I have no quarrel with the press coverage I got in the minor leagues—even when I was getting bombed—nor the coverage I had in Oakland or Atlanta or Washington.

I do have a quarrel with the coverage the Washington writers gave Ted Williams. They were scared to death of him, and one of them admitted as much to me. I asked why the writers and broadcasters didn't get on Williams, and the answer I got was:

"Williams is great copy. He intimidates us, and if we knock him at all, he'll shut us out and refuse to talk with us. We have a good thing going and we can't afford to screw it up."

That, my friends, is unfortunate: when a man becomes a sacred cow and is above criticism.

And the media is in that group—above criticism—because who is there to criticize writers and broadcasters, and more important, who'll report that criticism when it takes place?

There are too many Rona Barretts in the world. I met her just once, at a party at Marty Allen's home. It was a full-out Hollywood party and there were lots of celebrities on hand. I was impressed.

0

I met Rona, the gossip gal, and talked with her no more than three minutes. I came to the party alone and I left alone, and we didn't talk about anything meaningful.

No sooner had we gotten off the road trip and back to Detroit than Rona came on the air, on her syndicated gossip-gab show, and reported that Denny McLain was about to leave his wife for a flight into Hollywood-land with some starlet.

I was working late at the office at the time and didn't see the show, but believe me, Sharyn did. I got one of those quick calls to hurry home, and for days after that I tried unsuccessfully to reach Rona Barrett to tell her where to get off. She never returned my calls.

The main problem with that kind of reporting is that the victim has no defense against it and no way of getting even. And irresponsible people like that don't give a damn how much damage they do to a man's reputation and home life. All the gossip columnists and scandal magazines should be run out of business.

In the early stages of my career, I tried to live up to the fancy-free and footloose image the press created for me, and I deliberately tried to be colorful and quotable. No more.

It occurred to me too late that athletes and other public figures are essentially like everybody else, except that we lack privacy. And we move in a world that is largely fantasy, because it's a game that in many ways is so unreal.

LIFE BEGINS

13

AT THIRTY

. . . and if it doesn't, I'm in a whole lot of trouble—again.

Life is just starting all over for me. I really believe it. I know it's not going to be utopian and I'll have some problems along the way, but I'm a lot better equipped to deal with them now.

If nothing else, the harrowing experiences I've endured over the last half dozen years have steeled me for almost anything that could occur.

I pulled off a professional baseball uniform for the last time in 1973 in Shreveport, Louisiana. I hadn't spent a single day in the major leagues that season, except for spring training, and I made up my mind that night in Shreveport that I'd never pitch anywhere except in the big leagues. No more bush leagues for Denny.

My good friend Ray Johnson and I sat in a restaurant—a place called Denny's, as a matter of fact—that night after the game. I had ordered a chicken-fried steak and I asked Ray about my chances.

"You and I both know you can pitch well enough to win in the major leagues, Denny, and I'm certain we'll hear some good news in the morning."

The scouts from the Cincinnati Reds had been watching me, and next morning we got the news. It was not good. The Reds had decided to call up a younger player from the minors. They were in the middle of the pennant race. It was late August. I knew I could have helped them win it.

The next day I packed my things and left. I was supposed to pitch again in four or five days but all the stuffing was drained out of me. Ray understood. I had no heart for it any longer. I guess, in truth, I felt rejected and humiliated.

It had been fun working for Ray, pitching in Des Moines and Shreveport. It was a good summer. I enjoyed life and did things at my own pace and he treated me well. But he understood how I felt. Denny McLain simply could not endure life in the bushes for another day. I had sold the businesses in Atlanta and, except for our home in Florida and whatever money we had in our pockets, that was it. I had maybe seven or eight thousand dollars in the bank and no job.

So I went home to Atlanta. Some weeks before that, Detroit broadcaster Vince Doyle had called me and asked if I'd be interested in doing a radio or television show back in Detroit.

It was a little late in the game to play hard-to-get.

"Would tomorrow be too soon to get there?"

He said an attorney friend of his would call me, and he did.

0

He said the deal was all locked up and that I'd do a once-a-week television show. The sponsor had already been lined up.

I flew to Detroit and immediately went into a meeting with two executives from Channel 9. They asked if I'd like to host a hockey show.

"I'd love it," I said. "But I'd have to do some brushing up on the sport. I don't know the pink line from the green line."

They informed me the lines were blue and red.

See there, I'd learned something already and the show hadn't even hit the air yet!

Hell, nobody's perfect.

Our money was to come from commercials we'd sell. The deal was set, but nothing was signed. We went to Port Huron to watch the Red Wings in their annual press day at the opening of training camp. People were friendly. The prodigal son returns to the scene of the crime. Even Joe Falls said hello. My caps nearly fell out of my mouth.

Alex Delvecchio, who later was to become coach of the club, came up and chatted for a while. He asked if I knew much about hockey and I told him I knew next to nothing.

"Don't worry about it," he assured me. "A lot of guys who are playing the game don't know much about it either."

I immediately felt better.

I headed back to Atlanta to get my gear in order but, before I could pack, there was an article all over the country on both wire services denying that the show was going on the air. It seems the folks at Channel 9 forgot to clear it with the higher-ups and they queered the deal after it had already been set.

The attorney, Brian Smith, was as sick about the developments as I. Meantime, Brian had introduced me to Jack Rehburg, who was doing public relations work for Dino's Pizza. Jack was determined to put a deal together—and he did, at WEXL-Radio. We went on the air with a talk show, and almost as quickly as we got it launched Jack put together a television show at Channel 20, a UHF station.

They weren't the biggest or the most powerful and influential stations in Detroit, but neither was Harlan, Kentucky, when I began my baseball career. It was a start and I'll always be grateful for it. But it got too involved, with too many fingers cutting into the pie, and I could see the old problems rearing their ugly heads again—too many people, too many deals, not enough money. We were operating on a shoestring and destined to fail. Still, I became involved in doing public relations for several of the accounts and met some wonderful people who've launched me on a new career in business.

So I moved into advertising, promotion, and public relations and from there into some businesses for myself.

I bought into a place called the Trading Post in Roseville, a suburb on the eastern outskirts of Detroit. At first I had just ten percent of the action but now I'm in it up to my neck. We've renamed it the International Mall.

It's a giant fun house with about five hundred pinball machines, a place for rock concerts, a group of shops that appeal to the young crowd, and we have great plans for it.

I may even sit down at the organ and play some night, if I can be assured that the critic from *Variety* isn't in the audience.

I've found that the name Denny McLain isn't dead, that people still remember, and that most of them remember it kindly.

Through the television show I met some concerned people who are involved in drug rehabilitation, and together we've started a methadone clinic. It'd sound very lofty if I said I was involved in it strictly out of a high sense of purpose, because of my burning desire to serve humanity. That's part of it. I hate drugs, I've spent thousands of hours working in drug programs and talking to youngsters about the evils of drugs and I'm convinced the drug problem in this country is truly a major one and is largely responsible for our soaring crime rate.

But in all candor, I'm in it because it's a living for me, and because, through this worthwhile program, I can help feed Sharyn and my four little ones.

There's been a ton of work in trying to get the clinic off the ground, and the people in the Federal Government have been tremendously helpful to me. Once in a while, one of them will kid me just a little bit about the "other time" I was engaged in prolonged conversations with government officials. Believe me, the ones I'm having these days are much more pleasant and a lot better for me.

Once in a while, there are irritations. Sometimes when I'm having a phone installed, someone from the telephone company will demand a five hundred dollar deposit, saying "You're Denny McLain, and you ripped us off some years ago."

When I tried to lease a car, I got the same garbage.

I'm not going to tell you it doesn't hurt, but I try my best to endure the occasional darts without losing my cool. Most of the time it's successful. But it's a tough battle, reestablishing not only your credit, but your credibility.

Right now, I'm busy reestablishing that second thing with Sharyn. We're having a reconciliation as this book is being completed, and I have the woman I love and our four children surrounding me. They make the irritations easier to handle.

Regrets? A ton of them. But like the man said in the song, I at least have done it my way. When "my way" wasn't the right way and the legal way, I had troubles.

If I ever strike it rich, I'll pay my debts. But if I have not a thin dime in my pocket, I've already paid my dues.

The easiest thing in the world is to be a spectator, to stand with hands folded and watch those in the arena do their thing, then to say later, "I'd have done it another way."

I would have it another way, too, a whole bunch of times. But at the time the decision had to be made, it was a right now sort of thing and I was in the arena, not on the sidelines.

These days there are no cheers and I miss that.

There's no booing, either, and I even miss that once in a while. For a little while, I had the whole world right in the palm of my hand. Then I let it slip through my fingers.

So call me a "has-been" if you choose.

Better that, than a "never-was."

After all, nobody's perfect.

P.S.

I am most grateful to Richard Marek, who gave confidence and encouragement when it was needed, and to Ed Ahee, Hoot McInerney, and Bernie Mellen, who gave friendship that never faltered.

Dave Diles
December 12, 1974